Courageous Hearts

Soul-Nourishing Stories to Inspire You to Embrace Your Fears and Follow Your Dreams

Published by Inspired Living Publishing, LLC.
P.O. Box 1149, Lakeville, MA 02347

ISBN-13: 978-0-9845006-3-5
ISBN-10: 0-9845006-3-4

Library of Congress Control Number: 2017915307

www.InspiredLivingPublishing.com
(508) 265-7929

Cover and Layout Design: Rachel Dunham, www.YourBrandTherapy.com

Editors: Bryna René Haynes & Rebecca van Laer, www.TheHeartofWriting.com; Deborah
Kevin, www.DeborahKevin.com

Printed in the United States.

DEDICATION

This book is dedicated to ...

Every woman who has had to dig deep and find the courage to step beyond her perceived limitations and into the unknown. You are stronger than you know, and more beautiful than you can imagine.

And also to ...

Niki, my daughter, who inspires me daily with her loving, compassionate heart, and is a beautiful model for her own daughter, my beloved Little Goddess, Makenna.

Makenna, the light of my life, who exudes love, radical joy, and passion in everything she does, and inspires me to do the same.

Tyler, my grandson, my greatest inspiration, who has embraced his courageous heart after unimaginable loss to move forward with trust and love.

Dana, "My Man," who helps me find the courage to be my best self and do my best work every day.

The authors of *Courageous Hearts*, who spilled their vulnerable souls onto these pages for the benefit of every woman who reads it.

The extraordinary team of women who worked tirelessly to bring this project into being: Bryna René Haynes, Chief Editor for Inspired Living Publishing, who always knows my heart; Deborah Kevin, ILP's new Associate Editor, who dove in with total abandon and brought a new dynamic to our process; Rebecca van Laer, who helped many of these stories shine with her impeccable editing skills;

Rachel Dunham, the creative visionary behind the "look" of this book (and all my brands); Nichol Skaggs, my amazing-gift-from-the-Universe assistant; and, of course, Kim Turcotte, my Goddess of Operations, who brings my vision (and my websites) to life.

And finally, to ...

You, reader: whether you are just finding that brave place within yourself, or have been living there for years, you are a light in my world. Thank you for believing in my vision, and in this work. I couldn't do it without you!

PRAISE
FOR COURAGEOUS HEARTS

"With *Courageous Hearts*, Linda Joy has curated a powerful collection of inspiring life stories of truth-telling and change that we can all find ourselves inside of. Treat yourself and allow this book to be the catalyst that ignites the spark of boldness within you!" ~ Nancy Levin, bestselling author of *Worthy*

"Publisher Linda Joy has done it again with this compelling and inspiring book! Every moving story offers wisdom, inspiration, and deep support for following your own courageous heart—your own inner guidance. You will not be able to put this book down!" ~ Margaret Paul, PhD, best-selling author, facilitator and cocreator of Inner Bonding

"*Courageous Hearts* is a collection of empowering stories eloquently shared by women on a mission to inspire us all. Their personal stories illustrate courage is really about bridging the gap of fear and uncertainty by turning inward and trusting the soft whisper of our inner guide—we all have that power. ~ Emily Madill, author and professional coach

"*Courageous Hearts* is a must-read for modern times. Full to the brim with women who had the courage to tell their stories in service to others so that we can learn from their experiences. These stories tell of love lost and found, deep grief and intense joy. They are a rollercoaster of movement through the profound moments of these women's lives. If you love a great story or need to borrow some courage for a tough moment in your life, read this book. Every thing you need is here. ~ Minette Riordan, Ph.D., best-selling author and speaker

"Every act of empowerment, transformation and healing starts with a courageous act. This inspiring book is filled with the stories of women who chose courageous action in the face of remarkable challenges and transformed their lives forever. Each story has the power to remind you of the infinite possibilities that exist in your life when you embrace your strength and courage and take inspired action. It was a wonderfully nurturing and inspiring read!" ~Kelley Grimes, MSW Counselor, best-selling author, and self-nurturing expert

"Reading the beautiful stories in *Courageous Hearts* feels as if you're spending time with your best friends as they share their challenges and triumphs with you. If you're at one of those choice points in your life that calls for an extra dose of courage, then these stories will leave you feeling inspired and empowered that you, too, can trust your heart's wisdom and guidance. And who knows, they may even ignite a dream or two that your heart has been waiting to share with you ..." ~Tina van Leuven, Joyful Soul Business Coach, creator of "Money and Miracles," international best-selling author.

"Powerful stories by courageous women that inspire transformation! It takes great bravery, confidence and determination to take your power back, listen to your heart, make new choices and own your truth so you can transform your life. These stories are evidence that, no matter where we are in life, we can always listen to our soul's whispers and claim the joy, abundance, purpose and freedom that are our birthrights." ~ Patricia Young, transformational coach, podcast host,best-selling author and founder of InnerProsperity.com

"When chaos and challenge arrive at our front door, it's tempting to remain in a state of innocence in hopes that someone else will rescue us. But as the stories in *Courageous Hearts* remind us, WE are the ones we've been waiting for. By having the courage to trust and step across the threshold of the unknown, each of these heroic women unearthed their own strength and wisdom. Journey with them as they transform their lives." ~Linda Bard, Life Purpose Mentor, speaker, and best-selling author.

"I love that this book features highly inspirational stories and takes it a step further. At the end of each chapter there are questions allowing reflection on how you can apply the courageousness of the story you just read in your own life. This is priceless—as is this book!" ~ Jenny Mannion, author, intuitive healer, Mind Body Mentor

"*Courageous Hearts* is a journey of women warriors who, like many of us, have faced hardships and challenges that sometimes felt impossible to bear. These beautiful, sometimes heart-wrenching, personal stories inspire us to be strong with faith and resiliency. They give us the necessary boost to embrace our most powerful selves. ~ Dr. Jo Anne White, international best-selling author, speaker, producer, professional coach, and Energy Master Teacher.

"The stories in *Courageous Hearts* share with us those raw moments when women summon the courage to follow that all-knowing wisdom within. They share their stories of a choice to live this truth by taking courageous action and, ultimately, finding their dreams unfolding in front of them. These stories will touch your heart and show that there is such courage within each of us." ~ Laura Clark, best-selling author, Soul Wise Living Mentor and SoulCoaching® Practitioner Trainer

"If you've ever wondered what would happen if you listened to that faint whisper in your heart, these stories will inspire you to take that next courageous step. These stories of heartfelt inspiration from women sharing a range of grace-filled experiences, challenges, and triumphs are not to be missed." ~ Catherine Hayes, Enneagram and Leadership Coach

"Filled with stories of women saying YES when the world around them was telling them NO, *Courageous Hearts* is a book of inspiration. These authors show us how to love the world and, most importantly, ourselves." ~ Jen Levitz, Business Wizard & Coach and best-selling author

"Another gem from Linda Joy and Inspired Living Publishing! Miracles happen when you listen to the whisper of your soul. In *Courageous Hearts*, each contributor shares how they learned to face their fears, reclaim their voices, and carve out their own paths to personal liberation. This is a book you immediately want to share with your sisters and friends who need a nudge to follow their dreams." ~ Shann Vander Leek, Transformation Goddess, best-selling author, and award-winning producer

"This book is a wonderful resource for transforming fear to faith. Let yourself be inspired by these courageous stories!" ~ Amy Leigh Mercree, Medical Intuitive and best-selling author

"*Courageous Hearts* is more than a book about finding strength and courage when you didn't think it possible, it's a book filled with permission slips: permission to be you, permission to do things that work for you (no matter what anyone else might think), and permission to live your life on your own terms. May this book inspire you to take your next courageous step." ~ Dr. Mary E. Pritchard, PhD, psychologist and BodyLove expert

"*Courageous Hearts* is a powerful anthology demonstrating what feminine power is all about. These thirty brave women not only listened to their hearts but chose to move forward despite their fear. Read it to be inspired and motivated to make your own changes!" ~ Lisa Hutchison, LMHC, licensed psychotherapist for empaths, writing coach, and contributor to two *Chicken Soup for the Soul* Books

"These soul-deep stories will inspire you to reach deep into your own inner-being, finding the courage needed to meet the challenges in your life. The honesty is bold, life-changing, and life-giving. *Courageous Hearts* is a touching, sincere read." ~ Janet Nestor, MA, LPC, DCEP, author, intuitive communicator, and healing-helper

"I couldn't put this book down! As I read through every story, I was amazed at the courage and love exuding from each woman who shared her story. In fact, each story boosted my own courage. If these women can tackle what life brings them, so can I. Highly recommended!" ~ Jill Celeste, marketing coach

"If you want to be inspired to dig deep down for the courage to make the life-changing decisions, look no farther than *Courageous Hearts*! In this book, thirty amazing women bravely reveal their lowest moments and how they developed the fortitude to follow their true path in life, regardless of the obstacles. For me, admiration is too limited a word for these incredible women. They are way-showers." ~ Jackie Lapin, founder of SpeakerTunity.com.

"One of my most valued strengths is courage. This book gives courage a whole new meaning to me. It shows me all the unique ways that we are courageous and how we are courageous even when we aren't aware we are being so. We all need inspiration and if you want to be motivated to step out of your comfort zone than this book is for you." ~ Jennifer Urezzio, founder of Soul Language

FOREWORD

Kristi Ling

When Linda Joy called me to ask if I would write the foreword for this book, I'd just arrived in Houston to visit my boyfriend for a couple of weeks. It was one of those perfectly beautiful Texas mornings. A warm tropical breeze was kissing the Gulf Coast, and as we spoke, I watched joyful sea birds dance across the marina. We had no idea Hurricane Harvey was on the way.

That day, I thought about what I might want to say about strength, courage, and going after dreams. Little did I know that I was about to witness some of the greatest examples of these things that I could have ever imagined—and that, through that experience, I would know just what I wanted to share with the readers of this book.

Then came the hurricane. Those first few days were turbulent and frightening to say the least. Thankfully, the water stopped rising before it entered our place, but all around us was devastating peril and destruction.

We couldn't stay put. People needed help.

We spent the next few days wading through floodwaters, doing everything from volunteer search and rescue efforts to removing wet, muddy drywall, flooring, and belongings from the flooded homes of complete strangers who had lost everything. I lost count of how many times my heart cracked open that week.

On one of the days, we packed and delivered hot meals for families and volunteers who were hard at work gutting the ravaged homes.

I held back tears as we slowly drove through toxic waters down one long road. As far as the eye could see, there were massive, silt-covered piles, each of which had once been the entire contents of a home. Street after street, neighborhood after neighborhood, the front yards and sidewalks had all been turned into temporary landfills.

As we passed the school bus-sized heaps, I spotted the unsalvageable ruins of heirloom furniture, wedding photos, children's toys, handmade quilts, and other very personal items amongst the debris. These were not just things; these were memories. Treasures. Small pieces of people's hearts. Suddenly, the souls in this community were no longer strangers to me, but family.

As I watched so many people scrambling to clear out each home before dangerous mold and bacteria could take over, there was a distinct sadness in the air that I could feel in my bones. But, beneath the palpable sorrow, there was also something more.

When I tuned in mindfully and looked closer at what was going on, I began to notice inspiring signs that these brave warriors had no intention of letting Hurricane Harvey destroy their lives. In fact, many of them were making incredibly courageous, immediate decisions to daringly begin again—to dream again, despite their great loss. They were safe, and that's what truly mattered.

Some people even managed to find humor by placing signs on their giant piles of destruction that read, "Garage Sale" and "Yard of the month." Yes, there were tears and loss, but there was also hope, resilience, and tens of thousands of courageous hearts unified in love, kindness, and determination.

A week later, the airport re-opened and I headed home to Los Angeles, physically and spiritually exhausted. As my plane took off over the ravaged city that was now part of me forever, I thought of all those people below who were faced with starting over. It occurred to me how, just a few years ago, I too made a brave choice to start over after my life had been temporarily destroyed in a much different way.

When my decade-long marriage ended, I was broken, grief-stricken, and financially devastated. The life I knew, the man I loved, and the future I'd been planning were all gone in an instant. This was not how I'd imagined my life would be at forty. I had no idea what I was going to do, but I did know one thing; I had a choice to make. I could wither away into bitterness, or bravely face the heartache and fear that had engulfed me, and find the strength to rebuild and the fortitude to thrive once more. I chose to rebuild, and thrive.

Five years have passed since those first days when I felt like my life was over. Looking at my life now, I'm in awe of the courage, strength and endurance I've found within to not only survive, but also flourish! Since then I've traveled the world, written a best-selling book, created a new level of abundance, forgiven myself for some unfortunate mistakes, and learned to love and have compassion for myself in completely new ways. In the words of poet Kaci Diane, "I love the person I've become, because I fought to become her!"

It takes tremendous courage to start over or go after a dream. When a devastating life event or huge change occurs, it's not just about choosing to start over once, in one pivotal moment, but actually finding the strength to make that choice again and again until you're where you want to be.

There will be setbacks along the path. You may need to recover from, and learn from, a few wrong decisions, or huge losses that are no fault of your own. And, you will likely get to know yourself all over again through it, because by the end of the road, you won't be the same person you once were.

The incredible women who share their stories in this book have faced their greatest fears, survived great loss and heartache, and made incredibly valiant choices in the pursuit of their dream lives. I know you'll find each story to be a captivating and empowering read; a few of them may even remind you of something you've experienced in your own life.

We never know how brave we are until we're faced with unexpected loss—like the incredibly strong survivors of Hurricane Harvey and other natural disasters—or until the desire to change our lives becomes so strong that the pain of taking the leap is far less than the pain of staying put.

If you're going through a challenging time, working to build up the courage to go after a dream you've been longing to pursue, or just looking to make some big, positive changes in your life, you'll find wonderful guidance and inspiration in the pages of this book. Let them ignite your soul, and remind you what a brave, powerful, gifted spirit you are!

Whatever you're facing now or might face in the future, you'll always make it through stronger and brighter if you persevere, make daring choices, and find it within you to trust your very own courageous heart.

With love and gratitude,

Kristi Ling
Bestselling author of *Operation Happiness: The 3 Step Plan to Creating a Life of Lasting Joy, Abundant Energy, and Radical Bliss*

TABLE OF CONTENTS

CHAPTER TWO: The Courage to Live

CHAPTER THREE: The Courage to Evolve

CHAPTER FOUR: The Courage to Heal

CHAPTER FIVE: The Courage to Move Forward

Courageous Hearts

INTRODUCTION

Linda Joy, *Publisher*

*E*very woman has a courageous heart.

Our hearts are part of who we are—part of our beautiful feminine construction. Our hearts are our compasses, and they lead us toward the joy and happiness which is our authentic state of being. They are part of the essence of who we are.

The thing is, some of us learn to shut our hearts away, to wall them off from the world in the name of being "acceptable," or fitting in, or pleasing others. Other times, we simply forget: we forget how powerful we are, and that we have access to our innate, heart-blossoming courage at all times. We forget how to open the doors we've closed within ourselves. Sometimes, we even forget that those doors exist at all.

When this happens, courage seems like something that only exists in fairy tales. And so, we keep going about our lives, feeling a bit disconnected, or even trapped, never knowing that the ability to choose something more—something courageous and exciting and beautiful—is always available to us, because it's part of us.

At some point, we are all called to make choices—about our careers, our relationships, our health, and how we show up in the world. These choices determine how we create our personal realities. However, it is often not until we are at our most vulnerable, our most fragile, that we can hear the soft but inevitable calling of our hearts. What we choose in those moments has the power to keep us stuck in a life that no longer fits who we are—or ignite our authentic selves and open the way to a life beyond what we ever imagined.

What does this courageous choice look like? Often, it looks like the thing we most fear. When we are afraid to choose something, it's not usually because the outcome of that choice will keep us fearful and victimized; no, it's because that choice will catapult us into our power. It will make us visible, and vulnerable, and put us on a path to our own greatness. Courageous choice asks us to follow the soft, shimmering glow of our hearts, instead of the harsh but narrow spotlight of our thoughts.

The stories in this book are stories from my heart to yours. They are stories of breaking through the barriers we impose upon ourselves so that we can choose love and empowerment over fear and constriction. They are stories of love, of loss, of healing, and of surrender. They are stories from women who found the strength to do what their hearts were calling for, and whose lives, and dreams, blossomed as a result. They are stories by real women, for real women, and they glow with a beauty beyond mere words.

I hope you find as much inspiration on these pages as I did, reader. May you always find the courage to do what your heart is asking, so that you can tell your own story of courage to those who need to hear it.

True feminine courage isn't loud, or brash. It doesn't scream from the rooftops. Instead, it wraps us in loving arms during our darkest times, and whispers, "Be brave, for you can do this. You are meant for this, and so much more."

Are you ready to listen?

Bravely,

Linda Joy, Publisher

CHAPTER

One

THE COURAGE TO LOVE

MIRACLES ARE BORN OF COURAGE

Sheila Callaham

I sat mesmerized while a colleague shared her and her husband's adventure of adopting a brother and sister, ages eleven and twelve, from Russia. Just when they were set to return, they learned their newly adopted children had two older siblings at an orphanage an hour away. Unable to bear the thought of further separating the children, they made the bravest choice imaginable: they adopted all four.

"Adoption!" I exclaimed to her. "I can adopt children!" But then I realized I only brought half the equation to the table. "Except, I don't have a husband," I added.

"You don't need one!" my friend told me.

Imagine that.

I never planned to have children. It took five years of marriage to my first husband to find the courage to conceive. After growing up with dysfunction, I wasn't sure I'd do a good job. It turns out that being a mother felt so right, so perfect.

Following my son Nathaniel's birth, I developed endometriosis, and, later, ovarian disease. After several surgeries, only part of one ovary remained; this was one of the multiple reasons why doctors said I would never have another child. The marriage subsequently crumbled.

Not being able to have more children didn't bother me at first. But a few years later, as I watched my young son interacting with his father's stepdaughter, I began to feel a longing for more children—an ache in my heart and belly. Then the guilt started as I realized Nathaniel would forever be an only child so long as he lived with me.

Once I discovered adoption was a choice, I was on fire. Every day during lunch, I scoured the Internet looking for available children. In the year 2000, before exploitation concerns became prevalent, anyone could see pictures of children available for adoption and the highlights of their backgrounds. Whenever I read a story that touched me or saw a face that called to me, I printed the profile and put it in a notebook.

I learned from my colleague that the hardest children to place into adoptive families were older children and sibling pairs. Most prospective adoptive parents wanted only one baby or toddler. Like my friend, I wanted my adoption to make a difference where the opportunities were slimmer.

My search ended the day I saw six-year-old twins, Sergei and Alex. With bright and hopeful faces, they looked at me from the computer monitor as if asking, "Momma, where are you?" I knew they were mine. By that time, my notebook had almost one hundred profiles of children needing a home.

I knew I had found the two children to complete our family. The next step was to confirm it with the person who most mattered—my eleven-year-old son, Nathaniel.

I didn't even begin my search in earnest until I was convinced that Nathaniel wanted siblings. Even at the age of eleven, he was precocious. One evening after dinner, we sat down in the TV room to look through the profiles in my completed notebook. Sergei and Alex's page was strategically placed at the midway point. As I turned the pages, I asked Nathaniel to stop me when he thought one of the profiles sounded like a good fit.

Silently, the pages turned as my heart fluttered with anticipation.

Nathaniel's stillness worried me. Maybe he was having second thoughts. Perhaps looking at the pictures made him realize how different our lives would be with new children in the dynamic. Still, I slowly turned the pages, and my heart raced as we neared Sergei and Alex's profile. In my mind, they were already my sons. What would I do if Nathaniel changed his mind about sharing me with two new siblings?

When I finally turned to Sergei and Alex's page, I held my breath. I paused for the same amount of time as on all the other pages, providing Nathaniel time to look at the pictures and read the brief profile. He said nothing as he sat motionless next to me.

Heartbroken, I reached for the bottom corner of the page to move on. That's when his little hand came out and tapped on the page. "These two," he said. "They look like me."

Goosebumps covered my body and I silently offered gratitude to the heavens above. "Yes, they do look like you," I calmly responded. But I was far from calm. I was ecstatic with joy.

The next day I contacted the adoption agency in California only to learn that Sergei and Alex were to be adopted by a child-less couple in Pennsylvania. When I heard those words, time stood still. Eyes closed, phone to my ear, I was speechless. How could this be? I asked myself. I felt so certain they were mine.

I took a deep breath, opened my eyes, and calmly told the agent that if anything changed to let me know because I already had the money in hand. I don't know why I said that because it was a bold-faced lie. The words just came out of my mouth, from where I don't know. I hung up the phone and shook my head in disbelief. Disbelief that the boys were going to someone else. Disbelief in my deceit.

Three days later the phone rang. The adoption agent told me that Sergei and Alex could be mine if I guaranteed a certain sum of money to their offices as soon as possible. Only then did I understand the purpose of my fabrication. It wasn't *really* a lie. I had the money—somewhere. I just had to find the right bank to give it to me.

The first two banks turned me down because my mutual fund was not considered stable collateral, even though the value was more than what I needed. After the first rejection, I was shocked and angry. But after the second rejection, I grew fearful. I knew there would be no way to adopt the boys without a loan. At this point, I felt desperate. I turned to a third financial institution and came away successful. Nothing could stop me now!

I worked with an agency out of California, run by a man from Moscow. There were mounds of paperwork, translations, and contracts; then there was waiting, hurrying, and waiting some more. Adoption is not for the faint of heart. It is expensive, and adopting two children costs twice as much. Overseas adoptions are even more intricate.

Add to that challenge the complexity that comes with adopting older children. Now make it the first American adoption from an orphanage in a country where the law had just been amended to allow foreign adoptions. And with no American Embassy in Kazakhstan, the adoption required me to out-process through Moscow after going through the American Consulate in Almaty. The orphanage was 1,200 kilometers from Almaty. Almaty was 4,100 kilometers from Moscow.

To say this process was complicated is an understatement. In hindsight, I'm quite certain I was possessed by a fearless warrior goddess who ensured nothing stood in the way of my bringing these boys home. There was something within me that drove me like I had never felt driven before. The harder the circumstances became, the deeper I dug in my heels. I made a thousand phone calls to obtain additional information. I hounded the myriad agencies whose approvals I needed to expedite the paperwork.

When the time came for Nathaniel and me to fly to Kazakhstan to meet Sergei and Alex, I bought an oversized bra to hold the cold, hard cash required to "tip" all the agencies along the way. If I could get into Russian and Kazakhstan without my boobs being questioned, all would be good. My heart beat like a drum as I went through customs and my bags were searched. Fortunately, they didn't search my body, nor were there body scanners to reveal my stash.

The orphanage had arranged our first meeting around a noon meal. Nathaniel and I were seated at a table piled high with food. When the door opened and I saw Sergei and Alex come through, wide-eyed, I thought I would break into sobs. Instead, I knelt down in front of them and spoke gentle greetings in their language.

At that moment, forever imprinted in my memory, we began a new life together. One birthed by desire, made real through courage, and sustained with love.

Looking back, there were so many things that might have stopped me: expense, complexity, fear that something might be "wrong" with my children. Through it all, I had a quiet determination. A silent knowing. Whenever I fell into fear or anxiety, I looked at their pictures to renew my strength.

Miracles, I've learned, are born of courage. And when we love fearlessly, love flows back to us in ways bigger than we could ever imagine.

REFLECTIONS

If Sheila had believed that she "needed" a partner to adopt, she wouldn't have found her boys. Is something you believe you "need" holding you back from taking action? How can you shift that belief?

_____

_____

_____

_____

When you commit yourself, courage appears. What are you willing to do to make your dreams come true?

_____

_____

_____

_____

When was the last time you were (in Sheila's words) "possessed by a fearless warrior goddess?" What was the outcome of your fearlessness?

_____

_____

_____

_____

LOVE ON MY TERMS

Felicia Baucom

"I'm moving on."

He said those words with stone-faced coldness. I didn't understand where this was coming from. How did we get here?

Our two-year relationship had been progressing nicely, or so I thought. We had rented a house in Greenville, South Carolina. I had just met his parents over the holidays, and we had plans for him to meet mine. We were even talking about adopting a greyhound.

But one day, the energy of the relationship shifted: my body felt it. My mind wanted to rationalize it. Maybe I was tired. I was out of town often, working on a very challenging and draining software implementation three hours from home. I was also working out regularly. I danced with joy when my clothes fit better. But something wasn't right.

One day, my tears flowed non-stop while I drove to a local account. I still talked myself out of my feelings: *Everything's fine. It's all in my head. Probably just a phase.*

A week or so later, I arrived home after another work trip. When I pulled into the driveway, the cells in my body felt like tiny alarm bells going off all at once. I opened the door and there he sat on the couch looking sullen and serious. He said, "We need to end this."

He said I traveled too much and we weren't laughing, but I knew there was more to the story. I asked if there was someone else. He said no.

I tried talking through things, but he wouldn't budge. So I went to a friend's house to get support. She offered her place to stay for the night.

Somehow I managed to drive back home to collect a few things. I was relieved to see he wasn't there. Without thinking, I picked up the phone and pressed *69. A woman answered and I quickly hung up. My heart sank.

I wanted to be with my two cats, but I couldn't stay at the house. I felt like I had been kicked in the gut. More confusion set in. What happened? What did I do wrong?

It was the spring of 1999. The sun was shining and the flowers were blooming, but it might as well have been a dull and rainy winter for me. On the plus side, I lost more weight.

About a week later with the help of some friends, I moved out my cats, and then my furniture—which was pretty much all the furniture in the house. He wasn't home and he had no warning. I felt powerful.

I decided to move on as well.

I stayed with another friend for a few weeks before deciding to make another move. For years, I had been intrigued by Charlotte, North Carolina. Fortunately, my job wasn't tied to a specific location. After talking to my manager, I packed up my cats and my furniture again and moved to North Carolina.

The healing began the minute I locked the door to our old house for the last time, but I didn't realize how much more healing was in store for me. I left behind potentially awkward situations, but the sorrow and heartbreak followed me to Virginia, where I was involved in two long and mentally exhausting work projects.

Soon after moving to North Carolina, and despite the craziness at work, I was determined to meet new people. I put on a fun and friendly face, something at which I had become very skilled while moving around a lot as a kid. It worked. However, I felt hollow inside. I wanted answers: did he miss me, or regret what he had done? Maybe things had fizzled out and he was alone now. I didn't want him back; I just wanted reassurance that I was still lovable and worthy. I wanted validation that I had done nothing wrong, and that I wasn't doomed to repel men for the rest of my life.

I never got that from him, and it became clear that I never would. However, I kept showing up at work and social events, and I truly enjoyed myself. After about a year, I thought I was finally over the hump ... until a mutual friend informed me over dinner that the ex and the new woman were getting married. They had asked this friend to photograph the wedding.

And thus the spiral of despair began again. *How could this happen? How could this happen to me? How could this friend support them? It's not fair that he gets to move on and I still have no one! What's wrong with me?*

I read books, I searched the web, and I talked to friends and family. I called psychics and bought my first set of tarot cards. Once again, I wanted answers. Some were more satisfying than others. *His loss. You're better off. You settled. You weren't paying attention to the signs. These things happen. It's not your fault. This is an opportunity for personal growth!*

I'd feel some relief for a while until I heard more news of mutual friends getting married or a new love interest dating someone else. Sometimes I'd cover up the pain with more social activities. Other times I had no choice but to feel it. Fortunately, I found an online community of people dealing with heartbreak. It helped to know I wasn't alone.

The sting faded over time and I found much more fulfillment in my new life. I was laughing and playing with exciting people. I went on hikes and horseback rides. I tried swing dancing. In one summer, I traveled with friends to three different beaches. I had lots of fun despite the uncertainty of my love life.

Eventually I met someone, and we dated for about two years.

He practiced Tai Chi and studied personal development, which I was very much into by then. Once again, I met his family, and we had plans to meet mine.

Then something shifted. This time it was me.

As in any relationship, there were issues, and they were solvable, but I realized I was playing small. I had led a small life in South Carolina and, to be honest, it became smaller when I started dating the ex. My work travel, as troublesome as it was sometimes, actually provided a sense of expansiveness that I didn't feel at home.

Charlotte represented a larger life, and I had created it. Nonetheless, for years I felt that I had been replaced and that I was thus somehow flawed and unworthy. I had been so focused on being in a relationship again because I thought it would prove my worth.

I realized that I didn't want to hurt the new guy, but it made no sense to stay in a relationship that was no longer working for me just so I could someday be married, like the ex.

After months of going over the same issues, I told him I wanted to be alone. It wasn't an easy conversation, and we had many messy moments as I tried to share my reasons for wanting to leave even though he did nothing wrong. To the best of my ability I expressed my desire for him to be free to find someone else who could make him happy. I wanted to be free to listen to the clarion call of something else.

I embraced the part of me that craved a different life from the norm. I stepped into a larger sense of who I was and let go of the idea of proving my worth with a relationship. I decided I was enough on my own. Instead of searching for answers, I showed up with courage, playfulness, curiosity, and a fierce devotion to experiencing the wholeness and happiness I deserved.

I went to social events and chose to have fun instead of trying to meet someone. I focused on myself and created a life full of joy, adventure—and I certainly had adventures when I traveled alone to the Outer Banks, Boston, Phoenix, and the San Francisco Bay Area.

After the second break-up, I felt my life opening up even more. I still had everyday challenges to deal with, but by 2003, I approached my life with ease and grace. I explored a psychology program in California. I also noticed vibes of interest from Milton while we were traveling to a ski resort in West Virginia.

We had first met on a group hike a few years before, and we saw each other at various social events. We both worked in the technology field and loved talking about our cats. When he appeared on my radar, we were both available—but I didn't do anything about it right away. I enjoyed being by myself, and I felt the next step on my journey was to experience life in California.

Eight years later, Milton became my husband. I chose him because I felt free to be myself without needing to make him laugh or to fix things to make him happy. We're serious and laid-back. We enjoy exploring new places and things, and we're comfortable just being at home together. We have our differences of opinion and still come together in love. While my adventure in California came to a close after a few years, I knew I had plenty more adventures in store with Milton.

I thought my life was over in 1999. I'm sure that sounds like an exaggeration, but while I floated between hopefulness and hopelessness, that's truly how I felt. I created a new life for myself and I was on the verge of starting another chapter. When I moved past the end of the relationship, I stepped into a whole new life.

REFLECTIONS

What does love on *your* terms look like?

_____

_____

_____

_____

What long-standing beliefs about relationships, marriage, and your own self-worth have you brought to your past or present relationships? Do these beliefs align with love on your terms?

_____

_____

_____

_____

What steps can you take today to follow your own clarion call?

_____

_____

_____

_____

A TUMULTUOUS PATH TO UNCONDITIONAL LOVE

Kailean Welsh, MS, LPC

J esse's life has always been a whirlwind. I call it "the Jesse tornado"—it's fast, loud, powerful, and can leave a trail of destruction.

On day three of his life, I took him back to the hospital through a snowstorm because he wasn't urinating. After a slew of tests, the doctor concluded that my firstborn son was being stubborn.

"Stubborn" fit him well. As did exuberant, active, physical, unafraid, and deeply loving—all with a grin from ear to ear that lit up my heart.

Whatever Jesse did, he was all in. I can see his little child self plopped in a puddle, covered in mud, laughing with his whole being. I remember how he wrapped his strong little arms around me, using every muscle to hug me as hard as he could, sometimes so hard it hurt.

Curious and fearless, Jesse explored the world. He stuck his finger in the car cigarette lighter, burning his fingertip each time. He had an endless supply of energy. He wouldn't stop until his little body couldn't go anymore, so bedtime was a battle when I hit exhaustion and he wouldn't or couldn't settle down. Jesse was intense and emotionally reactive, once kicking the car windshield until it broke because I wouldn't buy him a baseball glove at a garage sale.

All in can be way too much.

Jesse was diagnosed with Attention Deficit Hyperactivity Disorder (ADHD) in first grade. Essentially, that meant that the frontal lobe in Jesse's brain, the part responsible for judgment and self-control, wasn't working very well. His brain was wired to constantly seek stimuli, but he had no filter. All impulse, he simply reacted.

I recall dancing one night in the kitchen with seven-year-old Jesse, his brother, Sam, five, and sister, Rachel, three. We were laughing and enjoying the moment, when suddenly Jesse enthusiastically launched himself into the air, arms stretched to wrap around my neck in a big hug. He slammed into me and we all went down in a chaotic and painful pile. Jesse landed on top, laughing joyfully, until he noticed that Sam and Rachel were crying. His smile crumpled. I choked back the tears, but felt them run down my insides as my heart cried.

Jesse was easily frustrated and quickly angry. Demanding and relentless, "No" was not a word he accepted. A trip to the store or a social outing most often ended with a meltdown, something broken, or someone hurt. His siblings bore the blows of his aggression.

I tried incentives, sticker charts, and rewards. He was talked to, lectured, punished, and even paddled at school. I grounded him, took away privileges, and allowed natural consequences. After several incidents of taking things that didn't belong to him, I told Jesse I would contact law enforcement if he did it again. He did. Sick to my stomach, I took a deep breath and dialed.

After one particularly difficult day, I went to Jesse's room to tuck him in. He was lying in bed, tears rolling down his cheeks. "What's wrong with me, Mom?" he cried. "Why can't I be good?"

We saw doctors, tried medications, and worked with counselors. I got a master's degree in psychology, wanting so badly to understand what was going on in Jesse's brain. Lots of people had advice. "He just needs a good swift kick …" was the most frequent suggestion. Questions and comments about my parenting skills and Jesse's difficult upbringing carried a veiled tone of blame and self-righteousness.

I thought about how much easier it would be if Jesse had an obvious ailment, like a disease or a broken leg. People would be more empathetic, I expected. There was no meal wheel when Jesse, at age nine, was hospitalized in a children's psychiatric unit. Few offered encouragement or support. I know people cared; they just didn't know what to say or how to help.

For fourth grade, Jesse lived with his grandparents. He dearly loved Grandpa, and we hoped special time together would be beneficial. By the end of the school year, my parents better understood. Mom told me about the day Jesse excitedly put on his new pair of skates. They weren't sharpened yet, but that didn't matter. For hours, he circled around and around. Mom brought him lunch, but he hardly ate. He had gotten started and he couldn't stop.

In his search for thrill, Jesse pushed himself to the edge. For years, there wasn't a photo of him that didn't show a bruise, cut, scrape, or black eye. I lost count of the emergency room trips, one a helicopter ride from a youth football game. To his teammates, Jesse was "Mighty Mouse"—small, but strong and fearless. He seemed to think he was invincible.

At age twelve, Jesse spent a year in residential treatment. There were more diagnoses: depression, anxiety, conduct disorder, intermittent explosive disorder, sensory processing disorder ... the recommendation was always another medication, often bringing serious side effects.

I blamed myself. For a while, the voice in my head was relentless. Maybe if I had taken better care of myself when I was pregnant, maybe if Jesse had a dad in the home, maybe if I gave tougher consequences ... Jesse once told me he needed me to be "more of a man." I understand now that he was asking for help, looking for me to control what he found uncontrollable.

I loved Jesse fiercely, but had a hard time liking him. We argued and said harsh things. He smashed doors and punched holes in the wall. I threatened to kick him out; he threatened to go so far away I'd never hear from him again. We battled over schoolwork and chores, about where he was going, what he was going to do, and what he said he would do, but didn't.

A college professor once said Jesse needed someone to be his frontal lobe. Good friends helped keep him in check; others took advantage. He went along with about every crazy plan suggested. He broke a kid's bike when he pushed it down a steep flight of stairs; he lit fireworks in town illegally; and he grabbed money from the carny at the fair. While his "friends" got a good laugh, Jesse got a reputation.

Unexpectedly, I gained strength. It's a tricky line to walk, standing up for someone who's done wrong. Jesse needed to be held responsible for what he did, but it wasn't fair that he was always the fall guy. I had to insist, "It was not just Jesse."

I wanted people to like him, and to comment about what a good kid he was. I got a taste of that through sports. Jesse was a good athlete: dynamic, and fun to watch. He thrived on the positive attention, but couldn't always manage the intensity. I was embarrassed when he went nose-to-nose with the football official, and was ashamed when he punched another baseball player.

I used to joke, "Every day that I keep Jesse alive and out of jail is a good day." Over time, the humor faded. Not long after high school graduation, the bad day came.

The heartbreak brought a fresh perspective. As the steel door clanged shut, I discovered one great undeniable truth: under the anger, sadness, guilt, and shame I'd been stuck in for so long, I loved Jesse, deeply and undeniably.

It is easy to talk about loving someone unconditionally. It takes courage to put that love into action.

I quit trying to make Jesse fit expectations—mine and

everyone else's. I made a conscious decision to accept him as-is. I focused on his strengths: he is fun, loyal, amazingly resilient, and compassionate; he has an eye for the underdog, and a fierce desire for a better life. Moving past guilt and shame into honest self-appraisal, I took responsibility for my part in our relationship. I set boundaries not to control Jesse's behavior, but for my own self-care. I stopped paying his bills, no matter how "desperate," and I don't try to fix it when he's hurting. I encourage him and let him know I believe in him. I express my truth, yet recognize when I've said enough. The rest is up to Jesse.

Looking through eyes of love, I see Jesse's heart. I see his courage as he trudges on despite hardship, struggles to believe in himself when others have given up, and walks through the fear that goes with being held accountable. I've come to trust that Jesse has his own path, and a soul purpose that I may not fully understand.

I don't know what's ahead. Each day, as best I can, I offer love. It's the only real power I have. And I hold onto faith, knowing that, ultimately, Light always shines in the darkness. Eventually, love will lead Jesse home.

REFLECTIONS

What does unconditional love mean to you?

_____

_____

_____

_____

Are there relationships in your life that could be better nurtured by accepting them exactly as they are?

_____

_____

_____

_____

Often, when we struggle to offer unconditional love to others, it's because we are also judging ourselves. How can you love yourself unconditionally in order to be able to love others in the same way?

_____

_____

_____

_____

WALKING THROUGH FEAR

Shelley Riutta, MSE, LPC

I prayed to the Archangels: "Archangel Michael, Archangel Gabriel, Archangel Rafael—show me the way! Show me my right path!"

I was lying next to my fiancé, so unclear on what to do about our relationship. I had been unhappy and struggling for months. I wanted a life rich with community and connection; that was not a high priority for him. At my sister's wedding a few months earlier, he had barely participated in the festivities. This revealed the deep misalignment that was causing my heart to hurt.

A few months later, I was in Northern California visiting my dear friend, Shellie, and her partner, Jim. Shellie and I stayed up late into the night talking about my relationship. I hadn't shared how I was feeling with anyone in my life, and it was such a relief to talk with her. I told her I wanted to stay in the relationship and work through issues that were coming up, but the major misalignments kept challenging me.

Shellie shared with me from her wise, knowing self: "Shelley, there definitely are things to work on in relationships. Jim and I have certainly worked on our issues, too—but what you are talking about seems much larger than that." I had observed how connected, joyful, and loving she and Jim were with each other. I was experiencing a powerful demonstration of the kind of loving, healthy relationship I knew in my heart I wanted to create.

The next night, I searched the Internet for some emotional support to help me navigate my next steps in the relationship. I found a coach named Liesel who specialized in helping women connect with their soulmates. She worked on the energetic level. I felt a connection as I looked at her bright, joyful face on her website. I could sense her wisdom, kindness, intuition, and strength. I sent an e-mail to her to connect. Finally, I was starting to feel some hope for my situation.

I traveled back home to Wisconsin and scheduled a call with Liesel to see if she could help me.

Before our first call, I waited nervously. I wanted privacy, but my fiancé was at home, so I was sitting in my car to get it. I didn't know what to expect—but once Liesel and I started talking, the words came spilling out as I described the details of my struggle. I had committed to my fiancé, and we had bought a house together. I was a person who kept my commitments. I was struggling with both the pain of being in a difficult relationship and the guilt of considering leaving it.

Liesel was present and understanding: she proposed that the first part of our work together would be sorting out what to do with my current relationship. She then asked, "What do you ultimately want to be experiencing? What is your vision for your life?"

That was a difficult question. For months, I had just been trying to keep my head above water. Vision—what was the vision for my life and my relationship?

There was a long pause. I felt so far from tapping into a different vision of what I truly wanted; I was in a black hole searching for a glimpse of light. With her encouragement to tune into the deepest part of myself, I shared the first glimmers of what I really wanted. "I want more connection, more laughter, more alignment with a partner who shares my vision for life. I want more ease and joy and lightness of being."

I knew that Liesel had struggled for many years with difficult relationships, and had made the inner shifts to meet her soulmate.

Now, she had been with him for ten years. She listened intently and was confident that my vision was possible. In that moment, though, I felt like I was far away from that vision.

We began our work together, and it was the most challenging inner work that I have ever done. We went deep to clear patterns of caretaking and giving up my own needs for others. In addition, I lacked the belief that I could create what I really wanted in my intimate relationships. This shocked me: the work that I do with my clients is about creating their deepest dreams for their holistic businesses and lives. It was hard to accept that I lacked belief about my intimate relationships—but I had seen generations of women in my family fail to create the relationships of their dreams. My family patterns taught me that true love just did not come easily.

With each session, I felt more clear and confident about what I really wanted and what I needed to do. I decided that I wanted to be free to meet my soulmate—someone who was aligned with the deepest part of me and the vision for my life.

The breakup was very difficult and scary. It took courage for me to leave a relationship that I had committed to so deeply, and to risk hurting my fiancé. I questioned, "Will I ever find love again?" As we prepared to sell the house, I found an apartment to rent nearby, and was soon living on my own again.

I continued to work with Liesel as I began to build my new life. Each day I felt stronger and more connected to myself. I had no interest in dating. I wanted to heal and feel on track with my life again.

Just before July 4, I received an e-mail from a friend: she suggested I check out a four-week Manifest Your Soulmate Course. I looked at what was going to be taught in the class and I was drawn to a bonus: the instructor was going to do soulmate readings. This is where she would tune into your soulmate and describe him; you could ask questions, too. I was so intrigued by this that I enrolled just for this bonus.

I marked my calendar for the call on Soulmate Readings; it was during the Fourth of July holiday weekend, and I was in Minnesota visiting my brother and his family. I told them that I had an important call, and went to dial in.

My heart was racing as it came to my turn for the reading. She began, "Oh, I love how the energy is between the two of you, it is so wonderful. He has a nice, masculine energy." I asked her about the masculine energy, and she said, "He has this martial arts energy."

I asked, "Do I know him?"

She replied, "You don't know him, but you will meet him soon: you both are ready to meet each other."

I thought to myself, *She is* so *off here. I am not ready at all.* So I shrugged off the reading and went back to enjoying the rest of the weekend with my family.

A month later, I was working with Liesel on a plan to build more social connections. I had lived in Wisconsin for five years, but I had been so busy with business, travel, and my former relationship that I hadn't fostered many friendships. We decided that I would start attending spiritual Meetups to seek out possible friendships. One August evening, I walked into a Meetup at the Unity Church and sat down in the only open seat next to a friendly-looking man. After the meeting, we began talking, and I found out he had been studying Martial Arts for thirty years. We had an easy connection and so many shared interests.

We made a plan to get together for dinner. I was hesitant to go, but I talked with Liesel who encouraged me to stay open and see what happened. I remembered my soulmate reading: I had been told I was ready. Could this be true? I would have to open myself up to find out.

I walked into the restaurant and surprised myself by giving him a big hug. From the moment we sat down, the conversation just flowed. I felt like we were long lost friends reconnecting. It was so easy, and so fun. We talked and talked, and marveled at how comfortable it was to be together. He asked "Don't I know you? I must know you, it feels like we've met before." Even though I felt I wasn't ready to date, I thought, *I can do this. This is easy!*

We have been together ever since.

The first few months of dating felt surreal; we would ask each other, "Is this really happening? Are we really together, and feeling so wonderful?" We have so much fun, and are connected on so many levels. All of what I wanted in my vision for a relationship, we share.

We were out for dinner the other night and the waitress came up to us and said, "Can I just share that the two of you are *so* adorable? You are having so much fun together—it is wonderful to see!"

Now, I reach back in time to the afraid, sad, confused me that was praying in bed late at night, and whisper into her ear, "Everything is going to be all right, my dear. Have courage to walk through your fear. There is so much love and joy waiting for you on the other side—so take my hand, and trust me!"

REFLECTIONS

When you tune into the deepest part of yourself, what do you find you want to create?

_____

_____

_____

_____

Shelley had to let go of her old relationship in order to make room for her soulmate to enter her life. What can you let go of in your own life to make way for something even more amazing?

_____

_____

_____

_____

What are you willing to risk to create the life you really want?

_____

_____

_____

_____

FINDING THE COURAGE TO FORGIVE

Kimberly Tobin

*T*hey say ignorance is bliss, but knowledge takes courage. I don't know who "they" are, but I never really believed that. How could a person not want to know something? How could she just stick her head in the sand and remain unable to move forward?

What I do know is this: be careful what you ask for.

It's 9:30 p.m. on a Wednesday night. Hubby is in the shower and I'm reading, getting ready to fall asleep. His phone goes off—a text alert. Usually I wouldn't bother with his text messages, but he's received three very quickly. I think something is wrong, so, I grab his phone and read his texts. One is from a co-worker asking about work the next day. Then I notice a name in his phone that I don't recognize. A guy's name. No big deal, I think. Then I read the messages.

I read, and then I see: there are pictures contained in the text, and they are not from a guy! Although they aren't inappropriate pictures, they are not pictures a female sends to a married man. Nor are the texts something that you would send to someone who's just a friend.

Then I notice the times the text were sent. My husband texts me first thing every day to say good morning and that he loves me. He also sends her texts, telling her to have a good day, asking what she has planned, and at the end of the day, asking how her day went.

Hubby steps out of the shower and opens the bathroom door. I'm standing there holding his phone, and I ask, "Who is Steve?"

"What? What are you doing?"

"I said, 'Who is Steve?'"

"Oh just a guy at work. What are you doing with my phone?"

I tell him that it kept going off and I thought there may have been an emergency. "That is not a picture of a guy's shoulder telling you about his tan lines! Who is she?"

And there it was: the moment when I wished I didn't know the truth. He had betrayed me. How did I not know? I was aware that our marriage was not perfect. I knew there were areas we needed to work on. And I know I can be difficult at times. But I never expected this.

The next few hours consisted of yelling, questioning ("How could you?"), and excuses ("It's not like that; it didn't mean anything.") My heart was in a million pieces. I couldn't stay in that house with him. It was the middle of the night and I had no idea where I was going to go. I got dressed among his pleas not to leave and went to my office. I sat there for what seemed an eternity, contemplating how this had happened and what I was going to do about it.

The sun was coming up, so I went back home to feed the dogs and horses. Hubby was still there. He just kept saying how sorry he was. His words meant nothing. He said he never met with her, that she was a high school classmate. I was in such a fog, I didn't give a shit about what he was saying. I didn't believe a word out of his mouth.

I showered and went back to work. From my office, I looked

up our cellphone records online. I could see when they talked, for how long, and who called who. I could see how many texts went back and forth between them. He was texting me in the morning and then texting her. The anger was welling from deep within. I was not going to take this lying down.

I obviously had her number so I called her.

"Susan, this is Kim. You know, the *wife* of the guy you have been talking and texting!"

"Oh …Hi. How are you?" she replied in apparent shock.

I went on, "I can see from the Internet that you are married as well. Tell me, do you think what you and my husband have done is appropriate? Do you think your husband would approve of the communication? How would he react to the texts?"

"He wouldn't like it," she said.

"Then why in the hell did you keep doing it?"

"I don't know," she whispered. Then she continued, "For what it's worth, he really does love you."

"Well, that doesn't say very much about you then, does it? You know he loves me that much and yet you continue to communicate in that way with him, a married man. I suggest you not contact him again. And I also would recommend you tell your husband. I'm sure he would prefer it came from you rather than me."

I hung up the phone.

I went home early, as I was exhausted and not much good at work. Hubby tried calling several times, but I just couldn't listen to his excuses. I had been betrayed. I know it wasn't physical, but that didn't make any difference. Actually, it felt worse. I was pissed, sad, frustrated, and sick to my stomach. She was getting the fun part of him. She got to laugh with him. She got his good moods. I got to come home to him being grouchy—not doing much around the house or wanting to go out. I got to fix his meals, clean up after him, and do his laundry. This was not fair.

After a couple of days, we finally talked. He admitted that they had been talking for over a year. They had connected online and it went from there. He promised not to talk, text, or instant message her ever again. I told him that I had put an alert on his phone and blocked every number that I knew was hers. He said he understood. I told him that I didn't give a damn if he understood or not. Our marriage was over.

The next few days were a blur. I was putting one foot in front of the other, checking his phone, checking our phone bill several times a day. I was miserable. I was grieving, and in constant fear that he was still betraying me. I knew I couldn't live like this.

Questions swirled in my head: Did he really love me? Did I really love him? Was it better for us to divorce, or was it worth the fight to stay together? At first, I asked others what they thought. Everyone I asked cared about me, but they all brought their own stories to the advice they gave.

I knew I had to get out of my head—to stop asking others what I should do or how I should feel. What would I tell my clients to do? I knew I had to shut off all the voices in my head, and I had to check in with my heart. My heart knew what to do; I just had to trust it.

As I listened, I knew I wanted to stay married. But I couldn't be the only one who wanted that. And I had to get the answers to the questions that had been swirling in my head. I didn't know if I was ready to hear the honest answers, but knew I had to know if we were going to move forward.

As we talked, there was one thing that was clear: I had to forgive him.

Forgiveness is a tough thing. Forgiveness was not for him; it was for me. I couldn't live in a constant state of fear: fear of him betraying me again, lying to me, and breaking my heart again. I didn't agree with what he did; that's not what forgiveness is. To me, to forgive someone is to set me free. It frees me from the burden of fear. Whether we stayed together or not, I had to forgive him and myself.

I didn't find a magic pill to just forget what had happened. I worked through the grief one step at a time, sometimes one moment at a time. I looked inward and found ways to be a better person, to know myself better. I knew I did not have the power to change him, only the power to change myself.

Throughout this whole time, not once did I consider that I was being courageous. I was just following my heart. Your mind is for gathering facts; your heart is for making decisions. I believe God speaks through your heart. If I was going to trust my connection to Spirit to guide me on my path, I was going to have to have the faith that God was going to lead me through this too.

We continue to work on our marriage. Eighteen years is a long time to just give up on. One thing is for sure: our marriage was over. Thankfully, our marriage as it was is no longer. We are stronger, closer, and more in love than we were before. Ignorance may be bliss, but knowledge takes courage.

REFLECTIONS

What does forgiveness mean to you? Who do you do it for?

_____

_____

_____

_____

Is there a person—maybe even yourself—who you need to forgive in order to move on from an old pattern?

_____

_____

_____

_____

What steps can you take to listen to your heart and begin the process of forgiveness?

_____

_____

_____

_____

FINDING MY HOME

Nicole Wettemann

"I am moving out."

The words hit me with such force that morning that I needed to sit down to keep from falling. So unimaginable to me, that it took a few moments for the gravity of these words to settle in. Only three weeks earlier, we'd moved into our new home. Unpacked boxes were still stacked in the garage.

As I struggled to grasp her words, all I could mutter was, "I haven't even had coffee yet."

Our relationship had been difficult, but the option of leaving hadn't been discussed so her doing so wasn't on my radar at all. Our relationship had not developed under the easiest of circumstances and was fraught with some difficulties throughout. I felt a deep love, a sense that we belonged together, and believed there to be a mutual commitment to make it work.

I had unexpectedly fallen in love with this woman only four years earlier while I was still married to my best friend of eighteen years and the father of my three teenaged children. My oldest daughter struggled with addiction. My younger daughter alternated between loving my new partner and struggling with the end of her parents' marriage. Despite these challenges, my partner and I made our relationship work.

We moved in together and often talked about how lucky we were to have found each other at this stage of our lives. Then, everything changed for me when I was dealt a financial blow, and my daughter's addiction worsened. I fell into a deep depression.

At the time my partner announced her plan to move out, I had just sold my home and begun treatment for my depression. I believed that things were going to turn around in our new home and that we would work through these difficulties together.

She felt otherwise.

On my first night alone, feelings of loss overwhelmed me. The emptiness in the bed next to me had an energy of its own. I cried like never before. All the losses and all the difficulties swamped me in my bed that night. A new beginning had gone abruptly to an ending. I curled up on my side and rocked, repeating the prayer I'd used since I was a young girl in times of difficulty and trouble.

"I want to go home. I don't want to be here anymore. Please, I want to go home, I want to go home, *I want to go home ...*"

Throughout my life, I always had this uneasy sense that I was somehow a fraud. I continually searched for a place that felt like home, while simultaneously believing there was something inherently unlovable and wrong with me. When I fell in love with my partner, I glimpsed the self I was meant to be. I felt liberated and authentic. In the good times, life seemed easy, love was beautiful, and my spirituality blossomed. I finally felt as though I had a home with her. Then, alone in bed, I felt as though the universe had cut me off from love and joy one more time and this time, the loss felt too great to bear.

With the prayer repeating in my head, I started running through the moments that had shaped my life. A difficult childhood in Germany. Moving to America as a teenager. Losing a baby. Mothering an addict. Leaving my best friend. Losing the love of my life. Slowly, I fell asleep.

Waking up the next morning, I knew instinctively that if I was to make it through this loss, I had to muster the courage to come to a deeper understanding of where this sense of homelessness and disconnection came from. I knew that I had to dive into the depths of my soul and learn.

I became relentless in my pursuit while battling the severe depression that had settled deep in my bones. Despite this challenge, I had a single-minded focus to learn about myself, my conditioning, and my story. I participated in silent meditation retreats and started writing. With the help of a coach, one day I recognized that I had indeed started coming home. I grew to understand that the home I was searching for in my husband, my partner, my children, and financial security was no home at all—that all of those things could disappear in the blink of an eye.

Through my work that year, I learned that my heart had been a silent witness, always guiding me along, its muscle tested in each of life's difficult moments. Waking in a hospital bed after losing my baby. The heartbreak and helplessness of my daughter's addiction. Looking into the eyes of the kindest man I know and telling him that I was leaving him—and then, only four years later, watching the woman I loved walk out my door.

My courage lies in the spirit of my heart, and its ability throughout these experiences to allow for the grief and heartbreak. To make room for sorrow and honor it. To see beyond the circumstance to the bigger picture. To have faith that these difficult stories wouldn't define me or my life. In my darkest moments, when getting out of bed seemed unimaginable, a tiny spark of a deeper wisdom encouraged me to move forward, not believing that the current pain or difficulty defined me, or that life was destined to be hard.

I learned that the home I had been searching for was within me. All the difficulties in my life had been signposts along the path of walking back home to myself. The size of my body, the shape of my nose, or the clothes I wear don't define my beauty. My worth can never be defined by the number of shoes I own, the size of my house, or the currency in my bank account. The people in my life and their devotion don't define my lovability. And someone's inability to see my lovability is not a measure of my worth.

The love I sought from others had been inside of me all along, planted there long before my birth by a divine spark. It can never be diminished, and no love given by others, no matter how profound or sincere, can measure the depth of the love I have for myself.

Today, my abundance lives in every moment. It lives in my daughter's beautiful, dimpled smile and the new ease of her laugh, free from addiction. It lives in the sweetness of the love I had for a baby I would never have the chance to hold, and in the kindness and compassion my ex-husband continues to show me by supporting my decisions and being there for me whenever I hit hard times.

My heart is courageous because I welcome every experience for the lessons they hold. My courage, which comes from the faith I have in myself and my divinity, is greater than any fear I have over what the future holds. Because I have the strength each day to feel the sun on my face and say, "What's next? How can I serve? How can I be better than I was yesterday?" Because I have the desire to keep on learning and expanding my consciousness—to follow the next signpost, knowing that I will be led home, fully inhabiting my courageous heart in my wonderful, amazing, heartbreakingly, and beautiful life.

One year since my partner's unexpected departure, I am no longer the same person I was. I live fully and joyfully. I relish creating new connections and honoring time-proven relationships. Now when something scares me, I give it a nod of recognition and jump. I know fear and heartbreak, and I've survived both. I also know that all I have ever longed for awaits me on the other side of my fear.

I am home. Wherever I am, whoever I am with or will be with in the future, I will be at home, resting in the love and peace of my divinity.

REFLECTIONS

What makes you feel like you are "home"?

_____

_____

_____

_____

What metric do you use to define your "lovability"?

_____

_____

_____

_____

Where does your courage come from?

_____

_____

_____

_____

CHAPTER

Two

THE COURAGE TO LIVE

BREAKING MY VOWS, HEALING MY HEART

Dr. Debra L. Reble

S itting on the wobbly first step of my back deck on a cold spring day in March, I thought, "I can't do this to myself or my children any longer."

It felt like my feet were on the ground anchoring me in my current life while the rest of me was spinning out of control into my future. At the same time, I felt depressed and stuck. I had long been unhappy, but had not allowed myself to feel the depth of my pain or to make an alternative choice. Yet I knew I was compromising myself by continuing to play the role of caretaker, keeping everything together to make others happy.

For over nine years, I felt as if I had been in emotional and spiritual limbo, going through the motions in my second marriage while setting my own needs aside for others. I knew this place well, for I had lived here all my life: waiting for the other shoe to drop, waiting for things to get better, and waiting for the courage to make a choice. I clung to my daily routines as a buoy so as not to slip into the sea of despair that threatened to engulf me. I knew I needed to lean into my pain and let it open me, but I was too afraid to do so. I also knew that in choosing to make my husband's life wonderful, I had temporarily forfeited my own fulfillment, along with my dream of genuine love and connection between myself and a true partner.

Lying on my bed, I was transported back to my living room on the night of my second husband's doctoral graduation party. I saw him standing, wearing a paper king's crown, and beaming triumphantly as friends and family congratulated him on his accomplishment. I watched from the shadows—not as his queen, but as a servant to his dreams, as always.

I had deferred my life for his in yet another self-sacrificial relationship. I had supported his dreams without asking for support of my own. In fact, trying to fix the relationship made me feel worthwhile and in control. I had created a familiar scenario—anticipating that a relationship would complete me— but instead of bringing us closer, our patterns of behavior had led to a situation where we led parallel but separate lives linked only through children and the house.

Even with my unrelenting love and support, he resisted doing his own spiritual work. He was content with his dependence on me and the stagnant day-to-day comfort zone of our relationship. In this graveyard of a marriage, trust, integrity, and intimacy were long gone; in their place grew a destructive kudzu vine of indifference that suppressed even discontent. I was living in passive coexistence of apathy and codependence.

From the perspective of my friends and family, my life appeared ideal. They saw a comfortable home, two well-adjusted children, and a marriage absent of external conflict. But what they observed was a facade. I tried to make my marriage work by taking care of everything, a deception that was encouraged by family and friends. They supported me as long as I tried to keep the relationship alive even when it had already spiritually died. Instead of listening to my own heart, I deferred to everyone else and their idea of what was best for me. Afraid of disappointing them, I had avoided the choice to leave my marriage, a choice I knew my heart had already made years ago.

Even though I knew in my heart that my marriage was over, I had tried to stick it out for my teenage son's benefit. I had already put him through the trauma of one divorce, and my heart couldn't bear to put him through another. I was terrified of breaking his heart, but most of all his spirit. Tom was only two years old when his father and I divorced. If I chose divorce again while he was sixteen, he would experience the break-up of his family, feel the devastating pain of loss, and go through the upheaval that a divorce brings with it.

My young daughter, however, was witnessing my role as a caretaker in a codependent relationship … a relationship void of mutual responsibility and personal growth. Did I really want this to be her model for future relationships? I felt as if I was in a no-win situation. What would I say to my children who depended on me? How could I tell them in a way that wasn't devastating? Any choice I made—even if it was the choice to do nothing, and change nothing—would end up hurting someone.

Because I had hidden my despair, Tom was shocked when I told him I was divorcing his stepfather. Even though I reassured him that he would stay in the same house and go to the same school, I knew he was devastated. There was nothing I could do to take away the pain that spoke to me through his eyes; yet I knew on a divine level that this was our journey together and that he would be okay. All I could do was trust myself and breathe love into him.

Having been told by her father that her parents would never get divorced, Alex fell apart in my arms the day I told her. So I picked her up, drew a warm bath, and held her tightly in our deep clawfoot tub until her sobs stilled. All I could do was reassure her that she was loved and that it had nothing to do with her.

This was one of the hardest days of my life. I needed to share my paralyzing fear of repeating my legacy of divorce, so I called my brother. Shaken by shame about the failure of my marriage and anguish over putting my children through this kind of ordeal, I opened my heart and shared my vulnerability with him.

As I spoke, I experienced a flashback to the day I was told of my own parents' impending divorce. My heart had imprinted the emotional pain of this past trauma, and it was now surfacing through my entire body like superheated water erupting from a geyser. At that moment, I realized that I was superimposing my own experience on my children. I felt that I was putting them through the same difficult experience—the experience that had haunted me for so many years. But as I talked through the connection between this past pain and my present situation, I realized, I wasn't my mother and my children weren't me. We were going to be okay because I only wanted the best for everyone involved. Exposing my deep pain and feeling supported through my vulnerability encouraged me to find self-compassion in the days to follow, even when things got emotionally intense. It also elevated my spiritual perspective and helped me see that my path was, in fact, my own.

The path wasn't without its rough patches. I had recently left my position as a school psychologist to become an entrepreneur in private practice. I had to refinance my house and buy out my ex-husband's equity in order to keep my children in their family home. But even though I had just left my steady job and had piles of debt from the marriage, the refinance went through on angel's wings. It felt like a sign from the Universe that I was being supported.

Before I could finally make the courageous choice to leave my marriage, I had to first forgive the vow I had made to myself that I would never put my children through this kind of experience. My heart was congested with feelings of disappointment, shame, and guilt for betraying them. Slowly, trusting myself and leaning into these layers, I sat with my pain instead of escaping from it into more distraction. I set aside time every day for meditation and journaling and faced my feelings "heart on" until they released. The more I released my feelings, the more I began to forgive myself for staying too long in another dysfunctional relationship. I realized I had made the best choices possible at the time. Trusting myself and letting go, I finally left my marriage—a choice that originated from the intention my brave heart had made that early spring day on my deck steps.

To create the space for a genuine, loving, and connected relationship, I had to let go of the relationship I was in and release the toxic residue left in its wake. Even though I was terrified of being divorced and single again, I knew on some level that I was inviting in an intense period of self-discovery and healing. Because I had always defined myself by my roles as a wife, mother, and caretaker, I felt untethered and uncertain, and questioned who I was and what I truly wanted. In letting go of my anger at myself and my ex-husband and forgiving the underlying disappointing loss of our relationship, I started to come out of the shadows of shame. I let my tears wash away a lifetime of unhealed loss. Like a cosmic cow catcher in front of a locomotive, I had to clear the track of anything that blocked the flow of love in my life. If I wanted to live a life of authenticity, I had to affirm that I was lovable and didn't need anyone's permission to be or express this love. And that, in turn, meant changing everything I knew about how to be in a loving and connected relationship.

The pivotal moment of inviting in real love and connection came when I found the courage to let go of my second marriage and chose to love myself more than the codependent patterns that had held my relationship together.

REFLECTIONS

What are your long-standing patterns of behavior in relationships? Do these patterns serve your happiness and well-being?

_____

_____

_____

_____

Whose well-being do you consider first in making important decisions? How do you balance your vows and obligations to others with the vows you've made to yourself?

_____

_____

_____

_____

What steps can you take to break free from old, unhelpful patterns and create the space for something new?

_____

_____

_____

_____

WALKING THE WALK

Ann Sanfelippo

I met my husband just after graduating from college. I was impressed by the fact he was a small business owner. It seemed daring, adventurous. Growing up, we weren't encouraged to take such risks. I was told to get good grades in school; that would ensure I got a good job, which would equate to a good life.

My husband and I would spend the next ten years working really, *really* hard to build the business. It seemed like we were always striving for this notion of stability, but often we found ourselves living month to month, falling deeper and deeper into debt. Our shared belief that "making money is hard work" was showing up as our reality.

This wasn't the first time I had encountered the belief that making money was hard work. It was ingrained in my family dynamic. I grew up in a small town in the Midwest, and in that culture, working hard made you a "good" person. The belief was that, if you weren't making money by working hard, you just weren't working hard enough.

Needless to say, this dynamic played out poorly in my marriage. We worked hard enough for ten people, but we couldn't seem to make ends meet, let alone get ahead.

I had followed my dad's advice and started investing in rental properties right out of college. My dad would say, "Renting is throwing away money. You need to buy a home. Then, if you buy one or two rental properties a year, and let the tenants pay them off, they will add to your nest egg." My first property was a modest duplex I bought right after college for my husband and I to live in. I acquired a couple more properties over the next several years, but that "surefire" route to security wasn't working all that well; we had vacancies, problem tenants, costly repairs, and every other issue you can think of. Instead of earning us money, our investment properties drained our meager resources even further.

Eventually, the stress over our lack of money and absence of quality time together led my husband and me to divorce. Suddenly, I was left standing alone, with nothing to show for all my years of hard labor but a mountain of debt. I was scared, and felt like a huge failure. My parents had retired in Florida during my marriage, and offered to take me in until I could get back on my feet. I accepted gratefully.

The next couple of years were a real struggle for me. I felt completely lost. I hid out in my parents' back bedroom, fighting a crippling depression and trying to think my way out of my financial mess.

I also realized that, growing up, I had formed the idea that a man would take care of me. The man in the relationship was supposed to be the breadwinner, the protector, the safe haven. But although my ex-husband was a hard worker, the business didn't provide. Now, alone, I wondered what was wrong with me, that I wasn't cared for in the way that my mother and other women I knew were. I felt like a failure—like I was not enough. My feelings of worthlessness only contributed to my downward spiral.

One day, nearly two years after moving in with my parents, I was making my way from the kitchen to my hideaway in the back bedroom when my mom caught me by my arm.

"Ann," she said. "You need to get out of the house."

I was shocked by her statement. *But where will I go?* I thought. *I have nowhere to go!*

She continued "You can't hide out in that room forever. You need to get out! Take a walk around the block, at least."

I didn't feel like doing anything. I *never* felt like doing anything but sleeping. It was as if I felt I could sleep my life away. But my mom looked so concerned that I nodded. It *had* been a while since I'd been outside ...

So, I tugged on my sneakers, put my hair in a ponytail, and stepped outdoors into the sun. "Just a short walk," I told myself. If I did the walk, I reasoned, I could justify why I was worn out and should go back to bed.

But then, something magical happened. As I walked, the sun's rays energized me.

Moments later, my life changed forever.

As I walked, the internal dialogue began. "I can't believe I'm in this situation. How did this happen to me? I *so* don't want this!" But then, for the first time, I stopped the inner tirade, and asked myself a better question—an empowering question.

"What do I actually want?"

I wanted to be out of debt. I wanted to be self-sufficient. I wanted to create a life I could love. I wanted to feel like a success—to *embody* success. *That* was what I wanted.

I was stunned by this. I had always gone about my life thinking that life happened to me. This was bigger than I had imagined. For the first time ever, I actually felt like I could control my life, and create the life I desired. As next-to-impossible as it seemed at that moment, it was something. It was a direction.

As I continued my walk, I watched the other people in the neighborhood walking their dogs, watering their flowers, chasing their kids. Most didn't notice me; those who did waved cordially, then went back to their tasks. No one stared at the girl who'd been living like a hermit in her parents' back bedroom for two years. They didn't care about my problems, or my pity party. They were busy getting on with their own lives.

On any other day, that thought would have sent me into an emotional nosedive—but today, it felt uplifting. I was done waiting around for someone to save me. No knight in shining armor was coming to take me home to his castle. No fairy godmother was going to magically take all my problems away. It was all up to me.

I finished my walk, grabbed my notebook, and sat down to make a plan.

I decided my best bet was to give real estate another try, and started attending local real estate investment meetings. I read anything I could get my hands on. If I wanted to do this right, I knew that I needed to learn everything I could, and put it to good use. I also knew I wouldn't see results right away, even if I did everything right, but I was okay with that. It felt so good to be doing *something*!

More, I stopped looking outside myself for inspiration. I surrendered to the fact that the ideals I'd grown up with around marriage, money, and my worth as a woman were not applicable to my life. Holding on to them was only making me suffer. Miraculously, the more I took responsibility for my own life, the more my fears subsided.

One night, I was up late reading with the television on in the background when something on the screen caught my eye. It was an infomercial for an investment system created by a well-known real estate guru. I was immediately interested. All my research had pulled me out of my rut, but the money wasn't coming in fast enough. I had taken on a part-time job to bring in money to pay my bills. This guru said I could create wealth if I followed his simple, proven plan—and I was sold.

The next morning, I told my parents about my plan to attend the local seminar and purchase the guru's real estate system. "You know it's a scam," they said. My friends agreed, saying, "Those things never work." But I was determined, and in the end, I went to the seminar alone.

That weekend, I made my second leap of faith. I decided to invest in a financial education with this guru and the mentors who worked under him. I put myself further in debt in the hope that I would learn how to get out of debt. After all, what did I have to lose? I wasn't getting out of debt doing what I was doing!

Immersed in this training beside other like-minded individuals, I realized that there were different ways to think about building wealth than what I had been taught. I realized, even more than I had that day on my walk, that I was 100 percent responsible for creating my own life, and that I had the power to make my life as great as I wanted. But in order to do that, I had to prove myself to myself, and get some results.

I stopped trying every new thing under the sun in my business, and focused on following the system I'd purchased and applying the knowledge I was gaining. Within two years of seeing that infomercial, I created my financial freedom through real estate investing. Not long after that, I was approached by the creator of the system I used, and asked if I would share my success stories as a teacher/trainer in his business. I would spend the next decade traveling the globe, sharing the secrets of my success with men and women from all walks of life. My modest couple of rentals was just the start as I went on to create multiple streams of income by building and acquiring other businesses. Now, my little enterprise has grown into a seven-figure empire.

Most importantly, though, I have found a greater purpose in my life, one that never occurred to me when I was hiding in my parent's back bedroom: to teach others that the keys to wealth, health, and happiness are already in their pockets, ready to unlock whatever doors are in front of them. If I hadn't learned it so completely for myself, I don't know if I would be able to share it as powerfully as I do.

Today, I look in the mirror and see a very different woman from the one who could barely muster the energy for a walk around the block. I have totally reinvented myself as a strong, capable powerhouse of a woman. I am the creator of my world, and I don't need anyone to provide for me. I am living the ultimate vision of my own success, walking my walk, talking my talk, and excited for the next big adventure!

REFLECTIONS

What are your inherited beliefs about work and your worth as a woman? How do you think those beliefs serve you?

_____

_____

_____

_____

Ann's life shifted drastically when she decided she was done "waiting around for someone to save her." Are you waiting for a savior in your life? What do you think would happen if you became your own savior?

_____

_____

_____

_____

What would it take for you to embody success in your life? What would that look and feel like?

_____

_____

_____

_____

FINDING MY HAPPY

Lara Jaye

For most of my life, I had a deep desire to do something great and purposeful, serving others.

One cloudy winter afternoon in Indiana, I was shoveling snow, feeling frustrated and lonely. Just a few months earlier, I had moved from one small town in Indiana to another to begin again. I was divorced now after twenty-five years—an empty nester slowly moving through a health crisis and building a new business, I thought for sure this move to a new city would be just the ticket for me to find happiness again.

Struggling to fit in this new city and to find my own purpose in life, I would intuitively hear follow the breadcrumbs of joy. Each day, I was open to where God would guide me. Often, these blind outings following the breadcrumbs of joy landed me on adventures down allies and highways, or to local coffee shops and boutiques, or to call or e-mail a specific person I didn't even know. I was beginning to follow my own inner guidance system for the first time in my life.

My youngest son was in college near me and my plan was to stay in Indiana until his senior year. It would allow me time with him in the summers and occasional weekend visits. We are very close: as his mother, I wanted nothing more than to see him through to his success. In the meantime, each morning I meditated on the longings of my own heart—living in a warmer climate, owning a beach condo, walking in the sand at sunset, managing a thriving business, having loving and fulfilling relationships, and enjoying vibrant health. I smiled to myself knowing that someday it would be my turn to live out my purpose.

I realized my heart definitely wasn't in Indiana, but I felt as if I *should* stay for everyone else. My parents' health was failing; my youngest son, my siblings, and lifelong friends all lived there. I was attempting to push through this short phase—then, I reasoned, I could follow my own dreams.

On that snowy afternoon, my eldest son announced he wanted to follow his dream of moving to Japan to teach English while he looked for a job programming video games. At the same time, my youngest son happily voiced his acceptance into the Berklee College of Music summer program in Valencia, Spain! I came face to face with the fact neither son was coming home to live with Mom ever again.

Although completely thrilled and proud my children were following their own dreams, I became overwhelmed and saddened that I was staying stuck in an unhappy spot. I had many unrealized dreams. *Maybe someday*, I had told myself.

That someday came the day I heard from my children that I was free to follow my breadcrumbs on a much larger scale. I got curious. I began traveling to where my soul led me. I followed the bits of joy laid before me along a meandering path. It took me to Los Angeles, then across the country to Southern Florida—Miami, Fort Lauderdale, and West Palm. Eventually, my breadcrumbs of joy led me across alligator alley to the Gulf Coast.

I felt like I was playing "connect the dots" in real life. Each crumb became a dot that connected to another and another and another. A purpose and plan began to emerge. A larger picture was forming in front of my very eyes! I realized each crumb was, in fact, a decision on my part to find happiness and joy again. I began asking myself, *What's the next decision I can make that would bring me happiness?* As I would go about my day, I would see many dots I could choose from. Each dot would take me in a different direction and connect to other dots I couldn't see quite yet. I continually asked God and His Angels to lead me to the highest, best places and people.

Once I had made a decision to move, my house sold in thirty days and I had ten days to pack and move. During that time, I found a dream beach condo on a Key near Sarasota, Florida, tucked away amid the sunbeams on a pristine crystal quartz beach.

The 1,200-mile solo move from my suburban bubble of safety became a stepping stone that catapulted me out of my comfort zone into an unknown world. Feeling scared and excited at the same time, I drove out of Indiana with a raging tornado in my rearview mirror. I knew it was the best decision for me. Visions of undiscovered possibilities of leading a fulfilling and happy life lay before me.

And, although I didn't know it at the time, I was being courageous. For once in my life, I was being true to myself and choosing my own path, no matter what everyone else said I should do. I followed my heart to a different location. My soul whispered to me, and I listened loud and clear.

I wish I could say that the move was delightful and that making friends was effortless. I wish I could say that I never cried myself to sleep from loneliness or that it was simple to plug into a new community. None of that was true. At first, I struggled greatly to find my way. I thought to myself, "Have I made a mistake moving?" People I met for the first time would say to me, 'You're so brave." Or, "Aren't you scared?" Yes, I was terrified! And I did it anyway. I was anxious, scared, and lonely. Regardless, I knew if I could move through the fear that was encapsulating me, I would shine even brighter. I knew deep down that I was being called to serve in this particular area, in some way or another. And, most importantly, I was following my own heart.

For the last fifteen years I've had a George Bernard Shaw quote sitting by my computer that reads, "Life isn't about finding yourself. Life is about creating yourself." And this is what I decided to do—to create my life and choose a happiness "dot" in each moment.

That's how I began to make decisions based on what made me happy, regardless of fear. At first, it was painful and terrifying. I only knew how to take care of others and make sure they were satisfied. Finding activities that made me happy wasn't always easy. Overwhelming feelings of guilt and selfishness would take hold when I first began focusing on my own happiness. I doubted I could be serving others if I was putting myself first. I decided to explore deeper the feelings that were bubbling up and clearly holding me back from living an authentic life. Instead of numbing myself or shoving the rising self-defeating emotions down even further, I would welcome them to the surface to be processed. I wanted to deeply feel them once and for all so they could move through me. My curiosity led me to name the emotion and its purpose in my pain. Generally, I would do this in meditation or by journaling. I wrote until the emotion poured out of me onto the paper. By becoming aware of the difficult emotions and allowing them to be, they became free to move on.

Once settled in Sarasota, it seemed each venue (spa, store, restaurant) I entered almost always led to meeting someone I connected to. On one such occasion, I felt led to go into a particular store. The unplanned stop eventually led to a workshop, book sales, an article in the local edition of *Natural Awakenings*, and eventually my own radio show. Because I followed my gut feeling of being curious, an opportunity presented itself to begin serving from my highest purpose—again, something I've always deeply desired.

A year has passed now since I chose to listen to my soul's call to move. I had no idea how brave I was in embarking on this move alone. I believe my soul knew where it needed to go next. It knew the experiences I needed to have and the people I needed to meet along the way. It led me in a perfect fashion. Living in this little piece of Heaven near the gulf allows me to bravely navigate the uncharted waters of my life.

My life is by no means perfect as I embrace daily struggles like everyone else; however, I push forward and find my happy. Today, my dreams are my everyday reality. I awaken each day to sunshine and the warmth of the sun on my skin. I walk in the sand of the water's edge while watching the sun set at the day's end. Yoga, farmer's markets, and fresh juice bars are among my weekly stops. Walking the Key fills my heart with happiness. The people in my life are there on purpose—providing loving, balanced, and healthy relationships. Outdoor activities like biking, boating, paddle boarding, and kayaking are just a few ways I spend my play time now.

My business has evolved and grown as I have. It has morphed into a brand with purpose serving others. As an international best-selling author, I continue to write, coach, speak, host a weekly radio show, and facilitate workshops helping others find their Happy and connect their own breadcrumbs to find a life of joy. Although some days are more challenging than others, I courageously continue to steer my ship of life in the direction of Happy.

REFLECTIONS

Where in your life are you putting off your Happy? What milestone will make it "okay" to pursue your dream?

When we realize our dreams, they aren't always what we expected. What unexpected directions have you been taken in when you decided to pursue your dreams?

What "breadcrumbs of joy" have you noticed in your life lately? If you follow them consciously, where do you think they will lead you?

THE GATEKEEPERS OF COURAGE

Lizete Morais

*T*his was going to be a good day! No, this was going to be a great day, I told myself as I took off the covers and jumped out of bed. Today was going to be the day that I would boldly follow my heart. I sat pouring my first cup of coffee for the day, playing the whole story through in my mind.

I'd drive over to the company where I worked as a corporate manager of training, walk in, and pass the friendly face who had greeted me for the past six years. After dropping off my things in my office, I would enter the human resources department, resignation letter in hand. I was going to do it.

I was starting my own company—and I would call it Authentic Pro.

It felt so exciting. But then the exhilaration and potential started turning into something else. What if I was making a mistake? The familiar voice in my mind whispered, *There's no going back. If you're wrong, there's no recovering from this.*

I wish I could tell you I was sure, that I had it all figured out. Truth is, it was absolutely terrifying. The words of my family, and especially my dad and dearest friend, came rushing back.

"Lizete, are you crazy?" Dad said from across the dinner table. I could see the panic in his widening eyes. Disbelief covered his face as his breathing grew heavy. How it hurt my soul to know that I was causing this anguish!

We had just finished dinner. What I thought would be a joyful, celebratory announcement had just turned sour. "But you love working for your company and they love you, that's more than most people get. You're going to throw it all away? Now, of all times, you are trading in security for some pipe dream? Have you noticed that the entire globe is in recession? It's insane— absolutely insane!"

Although I'm a woman of words, there was no sophisticated response. There was no logical, detailed plan. I didn't have one.

I sat there as the old familiar deep sadness flooded my heart. The people I love most in the world don't understand who I really am. They don't truly believe in my potential. They love me, but they don't get me. I felt the disheartening sense of solitude that I had always felt during my young life, and I understood that if I was going to do it—then I must walk the path alone.

We aren't ever truly alone, though. If we really look at the situation behind the emotion, we always have those beautiful angels in the wings cheering us on.

In my particular case, it was my husband of the time, who remains one of my closest friends. Although cautious, he said would support my idea for a year. Another special lady was a female senior leader who had become my first client. When I asked her why she was willing to hire me, she simply smiled and said, "Firstly, you're uniquely qualified for what I need, and secondly, you are the best trainer I've ever seen in action during my thirty-year career."

It was in that moment, sitting across the dinner table with dad, that I had an insight that would profoundly change the course of my life. I got what made stepping out with courage so damn difficult.

You see, many people say follow your heart. It sounds logical, and yet it remains one of the hardest things to consistently do for so many. To follow my heart fully, I had to face three gatekeepers of courage, and I had to face the vulnerability that I might fail.

The first gatekeeper I experienced was fear. Was I really good enough to go on the journey alone? What if it failed miserably and I landed flat on my face?

This was the cue for the second gatekeeper to show its face—the dreaded sting of embarrassment. What if I couldn't find another client? How would I face everyone if things didn't work out? I felt my entire body cringe.

The third gatekeeper of courage was about to make his appearance, and it shook me. I am a responsible, good person who cares about others: if I followed this dream, could I be blamed for messing everything up? I had a family to take care of and parents to support: was I letting them down?

Besides the three daunting and intimidating gatekeepers, one of the main elements that holds us back from starting something new is one question—are we ready? In hindsight, I know we never feel ready to birth something new for the simple reason that it has never existed before.

With all this doubt, fear, and shame running through my system, it was no wonder I had been in a constant argument with the voice in my mind for the last couple of months. But there was another voice, too.

It's not a voice that screams or has tantrums, but rather sounds like a constant gentle breeze flowing through the trees. It is a knowing that surpasses logic and intellect and seems to come straight from the heart. This voice would not be silenced.

This voice of my heart encouraged me to step forward into a new possibility, and it raised another question for me to consider. What would happen if I don't follow my heart? Is this all the joy, abundance, and fulfilment I could have? What if there was so much more?

What I understand now is that the real choice we are always making is: do I want to live my life as a whole-hearted person? That means living this life with your whole heart. And courage is the ticket to open the doors.

I did hand in my resignation—trembling, but I did it. When I understood what the choices truly were, I chose heart!

My business didn't just survive; it thrived. I had the freedom I had always craved, and being a creative entrepreneur teaching and speaking around the world came to me naturally. I felt absolutely fulfilled.

After around two years of running Authentic Pro, I was at my parents' home in Portugal when I got a very special call. A company in the Netherlands had heard about my work with authentic leadership, and they invited me to do a keynote speech at their special event. I was over the moon. I couldn't wait to tell my dad.

I ran into the living room where he was sitting down in his gown. Dad was deathly ill. The stage four colon-cancer that he had overcome just three years ago had returned with a vengeance. I announced it with all the enthusiasm of a little girl. "Dad, it's happened. I've just been invited to deliver a speech on a topic I absolutely love and they are going to pay for it."

I don't think I will ever forget the look on my dad's face or the mixture of joy, pride, and utter confusion that I saw reflected in his eyes. He was speechless for a long minute. He finally spoke and with a shaky and emotional voice said, "I can't believe it. I just can't believe it. You did it."

He proceeded to tell me a story that I had long forgotten. When I was six or seven, he had asked me what I would like to do when I grew up. He said that I had replied immediately and said, "I think I want to talk to people."

"Talk to people?" He questioned, "About what?"

"I don't know yet," I replied. "I like to talk, and I like people, and I think I'm good at it."

As my dad told me this story, he took my hands into his and cradled them. As he looked me in the eyes he asked me, "Do you remember what I said?"

"No, Dad," I replied.

"I said that no one gets paid just for talking."

I could feel the regret in my dad's voice and my heart broke. I could feel his heart break, and in that beautiful moment of perfect love, I saw the power of what it truly means to follow your heart. We get to set ourselves and everyone involved free!

The people in our lives love us, but it doesn't mean that they're necessarily right. The ones closest to us may not understand us fully because of their beliefs about what is truly possible. We need to receive their guidance as just that—their very best intention and advice.

As we find our way through the world, I hope that each of us will listen to the whisper within our heart. The call that we don't fully understand, but somehow know is ever-guiding and ever-supporting us to return to the fullness of all that we truly are.

Because I found the courage to live my heart's call, I now have the immense honor of helping many women, leaders, and talented professionals to remember or discover their dream and purpose, and to cultivate the courage to create a life they love. And it all was born from listening to my courageous heart.

I will be forever grateful for the moment when I truly felt understood and fully received by my father, because at his confession, he didn't have the imagination to understand who I fully was. You might not have been understood or seen yet either—but I know that your courageous heart calls, and I know that your authentic life awaits if you will only say yes. Safe travels, and can't wait to see you shine.

REFLECTIONS

Was there a time when the gatekeepers of courage tried to keep you from taking a leap of faith? What happened? What did you choose?

_____

_____

_____

_____

Has someone else's opinion caused you to doubt yourself or your dream? How could you reframe their opinions in your mind to feel supportive instead of limiting?

_____

_____

_____

_____

What would it take for you to turn up the volume on your heart's voice?

_____

_____

_____

_____

TO KNOW THYSELF IS TO LOVE THYSELF

Erin Esser

I tried to make excuses for the lack of intimacy within my marriage, the lack of true love exchanged between my husband and me. I tried to convince myself that this was okay and normal. I figured it must just be a phase in our lives, even though it had been a recurring theme for some time. I desperately reminded myself that I loved my husband the way a wife should because he was a nice guy, had a good job, and was a hard worker.

However, from a much deeper place, I felt empty.

For so long I tried to line up my outside reality to match what I dreamed for myself: a happy marriage, successful business, and an overall feeling of being happy and fulfilled in life. The problem was most days I had to convince myself that I was happy, that I was fulfilled, and that I was on the road toward success in my business. I did all the right things, read all the right books, and surrounded myself with all the right people—and yet, something was still missing.

What I longed for was to wake up with a fire in my soul and a smile on my face, ready to tackle the day. The reality was that I was developing a very intimate love/hate relationship with my snooze button. Most days it was an effort to get out of bed. Most days it was an effort just to feel good and stay positive. Why wasn't I okay with my life? Why didn't I feel fulfilled day-to-day? On some level, I just thought that if I became a better, more positive, or more grateful person, things would improve.

I distracted myself from my feelings and emotions by drinking. Wine mostly, because it's accepted and more glamorous than other alcohol—at least, that's what I would tell myself. I anticipated that first drink as I made it through each day. When I drank, I could escape what I was really feeling. I could ignore the negative voice within me, mask all of the emptiness, and forget, at least for a few hours.

I would curl up with at least one bottle of buttery chardonnay, so delicious it melted in my mouth, and allow myself to exhale all the worries and anxiety of the day. Some nights, I would couple the bottle of chardonnay with a robust cabernet, a treat with its chocolate and vanilla undertones. Of course, the white wine had to come before the red, because I felt classier that way.

All those thoughts I wouldn't allow to come into my consciousness went into each sip of wine, deeper and deeper, until I just didn't care anymore. There was a cycle: one night I'd drink to oblivion, and the next I'd feel like shit because I had a hangover. My morning hangovers riddled me with guilt and shame. I felt like I was in the clutch of a massive pair of teeth bearing down into my skull, making me plead and beg to feel better. From the floor of my bathroom, I would promise myself that I'd stop drinking as tears ran down my cheeks. Somewhere deep in my soul I knew that I was made for more than the agony I was living. I cried out for help.

What is my problem? I would think. Why can't I seem to get it together? What is wrong with me?

I vowed to stop drinking. However, the promise never lasted very long. I kept betraying myself.

From the outside, my life looked great: the illusion of a happy marriage, happy life, and great success. I hid who I really was from people, and even from myself. Underneath it all, I felt confused, like a nonstop battle was raging in my head. I couldn't figure out why I couldn't be truly content. All I wanted was to be okay with myself at the end of the day. Why couldn't I just be happy?

There came a point when I knew I had to do something. Either I was going to live a life full of regrets, pain, guilt, and shame—or I had to do something different. I stumbled across a guy on YouTube who spoke about being "the best version of you."

That's it, I thought. That's what's missing. I'm trying to be everyone else's best version of me instead of digging into who I really am. What is the best version of Erin? Who is she, and what does that mean? I tapped into the community where I lived and got the support I needed to grow.

I dove into learning about energy work, Reiki, and other healing modalities, educating myself on how to press into my shadows. I learned about living a life of integrity, understanding what that meant. Through this deep inner work, I started to embrace all parts of myself, even the parts I tried to hide away from myself and others. I had to examine and learn how to embrace myself fully and unapologetically.

In doing this work, I realized that by listening to all the books, the noise, and the chatter outside of me, I had drowned out my inner voice. I was not leaning into my higher self and my truth. I kept thinking there was something wrong with me, and because of that I would numb those emotions instead of letting them rise to the surface so I could examine and trust them.

I trusted someone else's truth, not knowing my own.

Since I tapped into my truth, I feel a sense of confidence and inner strength. There's power coming from within. I learned how to trust that still, small voice inside of me. I use my voice now to express my truth. I started a soul-centered coaching business to help women go from feeling lost and floundering to discovering their unique purpose in life. I get out of bed most days with a fire in my spirit, ready to serve and to live life to the fullest. I no longer need to numb with wine, and it's no longer an effort to be happy. For that, I'm incredibly grateful, and my life has shifted in a glorious way!

To be fully aligned in my own purpose, I knew I had to confront a big issue in my life that I was hiding from. I knew that if I was going to help others live their lives with integrity and authenticity, I had to shed everything that no longer served me as well.

On a Sunday morning this past March, I shed the fear of what I'd do if I weren't with my husband, and the worry over what others might think of me. I stopped telling myself that I might be overreacting, or that I needed to be more grateful. I no longer wondered if I needed to learn something from this relationship. I felt it was time for the truth. No longer could I ignore what I knew deep down: the time had come to end my marriage.

For most of my life, I've known that I wanted something more. I desired a rich life full of adventure, joy, and laughter. I believed that to have all I wanted, something deep down in me needed to shift. Looking back now, I realized that I wanted to trust in myself, fully and completely. Listening to the outside noise, the media, the church, my friends, and my family, and trying to measure my truth against theirs, left me feeling like I never measured up. You know what? I could never measure up, because it wasn't my inner truth that I was measuring against!

I don't know what is going to happen next or what ending my marriage will look like, and that is okay. For the first time in my life, I love the one person who knows what's best for me.

Me.

REFLECTIONS

Have you ever numbed your emotions with alcohol, food, or drugs? What was the result? How did you learn to confront and process your emotions in a healthier way?

_____

_____

_____

_____

Have you found enlightenment in an unexpected place—like YouTube, Facebook, Pinterest, or on a street corner? What changes came from this enlightenment?

_____

_____

_____

_____

What would it look like if you stopped measuring yourself against any barometer other than your own inner truth?

_____

_____

_____

_____

WOMAN WARRIOR

Charisse Sisou

*T*he smell of fried fish filled my nose. Hot tears slipped down my cheeks, finding my mouth's corners and mixing with my sandwich. Parked just feet from the drive-thru where I'd traded a handful of scraped-together coins for the furtive treat, I hunched in the driver's seat, chewing mechanically. Hair unwashed, tank top stained with breastmilk, spit up, and maybe a little pee from the last diaper change, my eyes were trained on the grass embankment before me. I stared past the sunlight streaming through the windshield, as oblivious to its beauty as my infant daughter was to my waterworks, her tiny body dwarfed by the car seat, head dangling at an impossible angle.

The depression that had hung like a gray pall over my life for as long as I could remember had returned, pulling me far and deep in its vicious undertow. I barely remembered what life looked like before its suffocating embrace.

Only weeks before, I had broken through to the surface and tasted my own warrior-like determination, choosing to birth my daughter at home despite a dubious spouse, a neighbor who judged me selfish, and my doctor father's alarming cautionary tales of exploding uteruses post-Cesarean. Armed with rigorous research and an experienced midwife, I held fast.

Sinking into my heels in the final stages of labor, I experienced firsthand the undeniable wisdom of my body. It was as if roots had sprouted from my bare feet, burrowing through wood and concrete to spiral deep into the earth, drawing strength from every mother come before me—while atop my shoulders swayed the weightless chain of all mothers yet to come.

Back cradled against a dear friend while my midwife lay belly-to-floor in front of me, her hands outstretched to catch the baby, I was supported by in-the-flesh women on every side. Even my sister distracted my son downstairs. Grunting, I pushed my daughter out with a pop so fast, and relief so total, that she nearly ricocheted off the bedroom floor, and I nearly split in two.

As I brought her perfect minute body to breast, her mouth agape, tongue already snaking for nipple, I felt as clear as sunshine on grass: *I can do anything.*

However, like the tide's ebb and flow, no sooner had my depression receded than it returned to engulf me, whisking my bright confidence underwater as it had so many times before. My body felt like a mountain, my eyes slit in rock, as my children crawled over me. Daily thoughts of suicide—as Ntozake Shange writes, "when the rainbow is enuf"—casually paraded as they had since childhood. It took all my energy to perform the minimum care required to keep us all alive. Hopeless as I felt, my children, as my siblings before them, kept me tethered to life. I couldn't abandon them.

One afternoon, as I parked in the fast food restaurant's lot to cry and eat, as had become my habit, it hit me: this brief window, between my toddler's drop-off and pick-up at preschool, while my newborn dozed, were the only moments I carved out for me, alone. I cried harder, feeling sorry for myself.

Abruptly, I was outside the car, looking in. I flashed on my sleeping daughter. And me, hoarding this scrap of food, this sliver of time, this narrow wedge of space, as if it were the only thing keeping me afloat. (And maybe it was).

In my mind's eye, I saw: the hot car roof. The sizzling parking lot. The city … Earth … all of time. And my life ribboning from first to last breath, one rippling potential path among many.

No voice boomed in the car or whispered in my ear. There was just a subtle, internal shift. A knowing, that came not from the self who cried into my food, but from a wise observer, who long predated the depression. Who had always been there, a quiet witness.

I knew: I had been here before.

The cramped, wedged-in feeling was familiar. Years before, when I was younger than my three-year-old, I huddled in a small closet under my bunk bed. My tiny fingers had pulled the sliding door of the closet as far shut as I could from the inside, leaving a slim, bright crack through which I watched the open bedroom door.

My pursuer appeared at the door and paused, eyes scanning, fist curled around a wire hanger, the sharp sting of which I knew well. Horrified that I would be found, I squeezed into the corner. Clamped eyes shut. Froze perfectly still. Held breath. And waited …

The closet door remained shut. The bedroom door frame, again empty. I had avoided danger.

A hush settled over me, my sandwich forgotten. In a moment of clarity, I saw how hiding had branded itself on my brain as necessary for survival.

And so I found myself, decades later, squeezed into a tiny corner of my life, skimming just above poverty in an abusive marriage, afraid of what lay ahead.

And hiding.

The connection clicked. I stopped chewing. My toes touched the silty bottom of depression's ocean, and I hung frozen, my hair floating like kelp. I was no longer that little girl. I had a choice.

I flexed, gently pushing. And chose to ascend.

It was not a steady path to the surface. I fell back into blame, into fear; let a thought or experience pull me under. But there was a persistent knowing that I could no longer deny—even as I argued against it, clinging to the safety blanket of my victimhood, my lifelong way out. Realizing that I had a choice gave me the space I needed to make the small incremental changes that pedaled me toward equilibrium.

Years later, dining at a long, rough-hewn table at a retreat in Puerto Rico, a woman who'd participated in my workshop earlier that day exclaimed when she overheard my suggestion that the way out of one's comfort zone is step-by-step. "I thought you'd be the last person to say take little steps," she said.

But baby steps saved my life. The first call was to a therapist. That therapist's suggestion to add regular protein to my diet, so plummeting blood sugar didn't torpedo my progress. (Who knew a cup of soy milk could keep me from teetering over the brink?)

That first yielding to my body's yearning to move. For years I had been sedentary, even though ballet was my childhood oasis. At the library, I searched for post-natal fitness advice and stumbled across an instructional video on bellydance. A long-buried desire rekindled: I'd once seen and imitated the movements of a woman I saw on TV when I was a kid—not knowing at the time that she was a bellydancer. Only knowing that she was beautiful.

Each desire dovetailed into the next. I practiced, then purchased my first hip scarf, its beads and coins glittering cheerfully in my hands. I wore it all the time, its ching-ching punctuating the sway of my hips as I cleaned house.

Gathering all my courage, I set foot in my first bellydance class … And though my body hummed with a sense of homecoming, I scurried away, scared … And then showed up months later for another class. And another. Then a workshop. My first show. My first troupe.

When I took the stage solo for the first time, the music started and all I'd practiced flew out of my head. I was so present, it was like an out-of-body experience: I was a vessel, and the music danced me. The crowd and the cells of my body cheered. My joy had found me. I had found my joy. There was no going back.

Baby steps turned into flying leaps. A new job stabilized our finances. Extra weight I'd carried my whole adult life melted off. I began teaching bellydance, then launched my first entrepreneurial venture, selling dancewear. I left a destructive marriage, and quit corporate to dance full-time—becoming an award-winning performer.

One day I looked up to realize that it had been months, years since depression had submerged me in what I once thought a permanent condition. I could barely remember what my life had looked like under its gray weight.

My body, my desire, and the same warrior-like determination that won my daughter's home birth had guided me back to the surface.

Back to myself.

REFLECTIONS

Have you ever clung to "the safety blanket of (your) victimhood"? What small changes could you make to change your perspective?

_____

_____

_____

_____

Has depression ever pushed you under its weight? What lifted you to the surface, bringing you back to yourself?

_____

_____

_____

_____

What baby steps could you take right now to start moving toward the life and version of yourself you desire to create?

_____

_____

_____

_____

CHAPTER
Three

THE COURAGE TO EVOLVE

THE OTHER SIDE OF "YES"

Stacey Martino

"I have to thank you, Stacey. I'm the happiest I've ever been in my life! You did this, Stacey!"

"No," I replied. "*You* did this, Sweetie. You did the work and you said *yes*! Thank you for letting me and Paul be your guides."

Tears welled in her eyes. "Thank you. I love you guys so much."

"You are welcome," I said as I hugged her. "We love you, too."

I grabbed my binder and started to herd the group together for the morning's class.

"Okay, everyone, grab some breakfast and grab a seat!" I yelled out.

As I walked over to get coffee and breakfast, I felt the coolness of the sand as it slipped off my feet.

I was lulled by the sounds of the waves crashing and the birds chirping as if playing a beautiful morning symphony together. As I reached for my fruit, I noticed the sun creating the most magnificent colors as it made its full appearance over the mountains and cast a gorgeous glow over the ocean.

8:00 a.m. in St. Lucia is a beautiful time of day.

As I turned around, this sight was even more beautiful. *Look at them, our incredible students*, I thought. *Look at their smiles. Look at them hugging and enjoying this magnificent magic moment together. Breakfast on the beach after five days of breakthroughs, laughter, life-changing moments and transformation.* That *is real beauty: lives forever changed!*

I looked at every face in the crowd and knew that they were happier than I had ever seen them.

Paul gave me the nod, and I began the morning session.

"Look around you. You are surrounded by some of your favorite people in the world right now, right?"

They nodded and smiled in agreement.

"This is your seventh power: the people you grow with. They will catch you when you fall and reach out the hand you need to get back up. They are the people who will also get behind you and kick your ass all the way up the mountain if you are not moving fast enough towards your dreams!

"And yet, just a short time ago, you didn't know these people even existed."

More smiles, more nods.

"Take a moment and look at yourself today. You are transformed! Every day you become the best and most authentic you that you can be. True or False?"

"True!" They shouted in unison.

"Now look at where you are. Surrounded by beauty. The breezes, the beach, the ocean … the majesty of the mountains surrounding the water.

I don't know about you, but I never thought my life would be like *this*." I felt a tear run down my cheek. "Did you ever think that your life could be like this? This is your life now! Take that in. Feel that.

"Think back to before you began your journey with us. Most of you were sitting at your computer or on your phone, staring at an opportunity to come to an event with us. Do you remember that moment for you?

"And all your thoughts: *What if I fail? What if it works for everyone else, but not for me? This is not convenient.* Your brain has an endless list of 'reasons' to protect you when facing the unknown. But your heart is still pulled.

"So, you harnessed your courage, followed your heart, and said yes to what felt like a leap into the darkness."

(Many more nods of agreement.)

"Tony Robbins says, 'The quality of your life is in direct proportion to the amount of uncertainty you can comfortably live with.' This is how you build your ability to find comfort in uncertainty: you anchor in the knowledge that *this* experience is on the other side of yes. The next time you are facing uncertainty and the unknown, you can pull from this.

"So, how do you know when to say yes? You must follow your heart, not your head! Your head is built for survival. It's designed to protect you. If it says mean things to you, that's not guidance—that's just garbage. Your heart is pulling you into the unknown because it's your next level. Your heart is your divine guidance. And yes, it doesn't always make sense and it's not going to be comfortable.

"It takes courage to follow your heart. Each of you had that defining moment before you said yes to this journey! Life will always hand you these moments. And what you do with them determines your destiny."

As I was speaking to my students, I easily recalled a time when I, too, had to walk this walk.

Years ago, in a hotel room in Fort Lauderdale, I went through a similar struggle.

Back then, I was still working my day job in corporate tax and coaching people "on the side" to help them heal their relationships. I knew I needed to help more people, but I didn't know how to let them know I existed.

I went to a marketing event to learn about how to reach people with my message. Going to the event was an easy decision. I love live events and I love growth, so I was excited to be there!

And I was right, I really enjoyed the event. The event host started talking about what it would take to get my message out there in the world, play a big game, serve my purpose, and let people know I existed. All things I came to hear.

But then something happened. She asked if I was ready to take action and begin doing what needed to be done to make all of that "dream" a "reality." She had a proven process, a program that I could follow. She asked if I wanted to join her program so that she could teach me how to create exactly what I wanted.

I started to panic.

It was more money than I thought I had to spend. It took more time than I thought I had to give. There was no guarantee that it would work for me. There was no timeline that I could rely on as to when I would get my first client. What if it didn't work for me? What if I didn't make my money back? What if it worked for everyone else and not me?

I sat there in our hotel room that night, crying to Paul.

In the end, I finally admitted to myself, and Paul, my big fear. "This is my mission in life, not just a business. I can't fail at this, Paul. What if I try this and I fail? What will I even do?"

Thank God I was with Paul Martino that night.

"There is no such thing as failure unless you quit. And you, Stacey Martino, are not a quitter. So you will never fail. I know you already work two jobs for our family. Money is still tight, and there are a million reasons why you shouldn't do this—but what does your heart say?"

"My heart says that this is the answer we have been asking for, this is my mentor and this is my tribe."

"Then you have to say Yes, Stacey. You have to say *yes* to the call, in faith! God has always looked out for you in unexplainable ways, Stacey, and this is no different. Faith is not an optional card that you can pull sometimes and not other times. Your heart is telling you the answer. Yes, it's scary. Yes, there are no guarantees and you are taking a leap into the unknown. *Good!* That's where the good stuff usually is! You are following what we have always known to be true. If you want something, find someone who has already figured out how to get it, has a proven process, and has taken many others there. You found her. You feel called. Your heart is telling you yes. You're scared shitless, so it must be for you. It doesn't get more certain than that, Stacey."

I listened. And I said *yes*.

In that hotel room in Fort Lauderdale, if Paul could have shown me the magic mirror with all of those faces of the people we would one day serve, it would have been a very easy yes for me.

But it's not possible to *see* what is on the other side of yes when it's your moment to make your decision. That's why it takes so much courage.

My heart already knew. That is why I felt so pulled. I had to follow my heart, anchor myself in the possibility on the other side of yes, leap into the unknown, and lean on my certainty and faith.

And here I am, years later, looking around into a sea of faces. All the families that we have helped. The lives we have helped to heal. The marriages we have helped to save. The children who are happier because of the work that we do.

This was on the other side of yes for me.

REFLECTIONS

What doubts, fears, and worries keep you from saying yes to following your heart's deepest desires?

_____

_____

_____

_____

What happened last time you took a leap of faith? What was waiting for you on the other side?

_____

_____

_____

_____

What do you want to say yes to this year—or even today?

_____

_____

_____

_____

BREAKDOWN TO BREAKTHROUGH

Marianne MacKenzie

*I*t was early, much too early for the sun to even show his face. And here I was, once again, at the airport.

Even though I had just awoken, exhaustion hit me as I left the house while my husband and two boys slept. I loved my job managing human resources at a Fortune 100 company: this was what I had worked so hard to achieve. I enjoyed busting through social and corporate limits and creating new personal bests. It was important to me to show to my boys that hard work really pays off. But I was too young to feel this tired. My weight had dropped consistently and my desires beyond working usually included a glass of wine and then my bed. Each Tuesday I gave myself a pep-talk: "I can do this … there are only three more days before the weekend … before I can take a nap."

To the outside world, I had it all. The family, the great position with the great company, a beautiful house, a nice income, a boat on the lake, a sweet car, and the list went on. However, the way I felt inside didn't match this picture at all. I couldn't imagine continuing at this pace in this way for much longer. I often wondered how some people did it: how did they show up for work each day? They almost seemed like drones. Was I becoming one, too?

Settling in for the two-hour flight to Phoenix, I reached into my briefcase for a magazine. I savored these moments: the only time I got to read a magazine was at the doctor's office or on a flight. Every other waking moment was occupied with deadlines, deliverables, requests, and demands. I took a deep breath.

As I opened the magazine, my eye was immediately drawn to the image of a lavender farm. This farm was created by a former executive and his physician wife; they were drawn to create a higher quality of life because their demanding careers had all but drained the life out of them. The article and picturesque flower-covered farm sparked something in me that morning that I didn't realize I was missing—a desire for something simpler. Beautiful. Natural. I desired deep, connected meaning amidst all the busyness of my life.

That article created a vision that not only awoke a craving within the deepest parts of me, but also sparked curiosity. Little did I know that this awakening had opened something big. Like one of those springing snakes in a can, once the lid was opened, this part of me blossomed much too large to ever fit nicely back in the spaces I had formerly known.

As the vision bloomed—living a simple life, connecting to the world around me, lavender—things started to change within me. I longed to feel the sunshine on my face in the middle of the day. Before, I had not even noticed the amazing view out the big picture windows of the office; now, I took time to go outside and take off my shoes to feel the earth. I craved fresh air.

One Sunday afternoon, I started feeling dread about starting another workweek. By nighttime, I was full-on sick to my stomach. The weight of it all felt over consuming: I gave into tears and feelings of shame for not being able to pep-talk my way through my dread. I thought that a good night's sleep would fix everything. It didn't. By morning, my entire body reacted as if I had the flu. I couldn't get out of bed, I couldn't imagine going into the office. My husband thought I should stay home, and after some debate, I called in sick.

One day led to another and another. Time seemed to be tricking me with huge gaps that I couldn't account for. I remember setting my alarm to go off right before the boys got off the school bus so they wouldn't see I had been in bed all day. I felt totally gelatinous inside, and wondered where all my drive and ambition had gone. The longer that I was away from the office, the more fear I had about returning. I sank deeper into despair and depression.

With much guilt and shame, I requested a leave of absence to pull myself back together. Certainly, this was just temporary. I *hoped* it was temporary. I felt uncertain and alone. What was happening to me? The diagnosis that the psychiatrist gave me was "nervous breakdown." The recommendation was to take anti-depressants. I took the medication, and soon found out what being a drone *really* felt like. I felt like a cardboard box. Soon, I took myself off the medication.

The voice inside my heart began speaking clearly and loudly to me. Was it just now beginning or was I just now quiet enough to hear it? This voice was crystal clear: I could not return to this life and work style. It was all I knew, and yet I knew I would not return. My wise-self became my constant companion as I moved toward restructuring my life.

During this transformative time in my life, I felt so alone, and yet so liberated at the same time. Suddenly, money meant very little to me. I realized that this affluent suburban neighborhood was not supporting my family's heart and soul. We didn't know any neighbors after living here five years. We didn't have the time to get to know them: we were too busy making money to support our luxurious lifestyle. It became clear that money is just a means to enjoy life, and clearly we had lost sight of this.

This new clarity gave me the opportunity to decide for myself what was important to me. So much of my life had been lived based on other people's desires for me. I learned that we live in society; however, we are free to choose so much more of life than we are taught to believe. More than I had been taught to believe. Through journaling, meditation and reading, I realized just how beautifully sacred my life really was. This awareness became the framework for how I experienced life.

This was certainly one of the most frightening times in my life. I was absolutely in uncharted territory and it pulled every ounce of courage I had to allow my wise-self to guide me toward what my head was telling me was foolish. Many of my friends and family members thought I had gone crazy. They all knew how focused and ambitious I was. To see me walk away from it all was absolutely "not Marianne." Even though a strength was emerging inside of me that was more solid than anything I had ever felt, I was being treated as if I was a fragile little egg that could crack at any time.

I didn't have friends that had been here before me, no mentors or guides. So, I found them through reading others' stories of courage to live according to their hearts. I found strength and clarity through listening to my own inner voice that had been screaming to get my attention.

It was years later that I realized just how sacred this "breakdown" really was. While watching a documentary on Joni Mitchell, I heard her talk about a breakdown that had happened due to her sudden fame. She had gone into a cocoon of sorts to heal, and spent time in the Canadian bush. She said that some people would call it a nervous breakdown, but a shaman explained to her that it was considered a sacred transformation— breakdown to break through to a new awareness of self.

It was in hearing this that I felt Truth. The shame I had felt for taking my perfect life and making a mess of it all suddenly turned into a sacred badge of courage and strength. I was a new person. The identity that I had created was hiding the depth of the person I really was. I am strong, and I am tender. I am loving, and I am fierce. I am courageous, and I am able to choose for myself the life I desire. It was as if I didn't know how to allow these parts to coexist. I was beginning to feel myself in a way that I somehow knew could never be contained by an identity again.

Out of breakdown and chaos, I decided to consciously live my life. I woke up to the choices that I had made and decided which ones I desired to make differently. As excruciatingly painful as this breakdown was, it allowed me to find my voice and to establish a personal truth that I began to honor. It gave me solid ground to build the big life that I had calling to me. I began making decisions based on my wise-self and feeling in my own heart. I constructed a business around my own passions and desires, working the hours that honored my body and my soul. These choices were not written in a best-selling business book; they had to be created uniquely for my life. My sacred life.

Many people didn't agree with my decisions, and often would tell me I was selfish for thinking I could live my dreams, or that I was delusional to think that it was really going to work in the ways I wanted. Well as the saying goes … eat my dust! The courage it took to listen to my heart was the same courage that it took to create my lavender farm.

And *that* story, my friend, will have to wait for next time.

REFLECTIONS

What are your highest priorities in your life right now?

_____

_____

_____

_____

Are your priorities in line with your deepest desires? If not, what steps can you take to align your dreams with your actions?

_____

_____

_____

_____

What parts of you defy "identity"? How can you make room to be all of who you are, every day?

_____

_____

_____

_____

I AM WONDER WOMAN

Jami Hearn

hat did you want to be when you were a child? An astronaut, a firefighter?

My choice was Wonder Woman. For a stint, I considered "rock star," too, until a family member ridiculed me for my singing voice. Despite the fact that I ended up singing on the world stage as part of an elite vocal group—and even shared the stage with Barry Manilow, singing backup to "Dancin' In the Street" and "I Write the Songs"—that imprint of someone else's opinion derailed my vision. All of the judgments offered by family, friends, and society piled up, and caused huge alterations to my self-perceptions.

Here's a perfect example: for years, I could not consider a career in the personal development industry a "real job," even though I saw firsthand the lasting and profound impact it has on so many people. I have a *law degree*, you know?

(And there it is: that voice of judgment that I learned from so many people in my life. Is it my authentic voice, or someone's imprint on me? Now, I'm ready to respond to that inner voice: I am a personal development professional who talks to and consults *dead people*! But for a long time, all I could do was shrink.)

One of the hardest choices I've made in my life has been to step out and truly embrace who I am. When I meet someone who asks what I do, it's like I've just shouted from the rooftops, "I am Wonder Woman!" People respond with, "Oh, that's nice. But what's your *real* job? Aren't you a lawyer?" And then they give me *that* look.

"Seriously," I say. "This is my real job! I teach professional women to find fulfillment through spiritual connection and the Akashic Records."

Talking to dead people is hard work, but sometimes, talking to the living is exponentially harder!

As a lawyer, I was depressed and miserable, caught in the gerbil wheel and going nowhere. In the traditional practice of law, a number of things were not working in my favor. First, I am a woman. Second, I have children (they call that the Mommy track), and in a business where the goal is billable hours, that's a big hurdle. There was a lot of pressure to conform to the "lawyer blueprint," but I couldn't reconcile my deep-rooted values with industry conventions created by people with whom I had nothing in common.

Seeking more heartfelt connection in my life, I turned to a friend who was an energy healer, and started learning more about her path. (Covertly, of course!) I spent my nights and weekends exploring the world of spirituality, trying to find a niche that resounded. I even changed my schedule to a four-day work week so I could devote more time to spirituality and balance.

My desire for balance was an insurmountable challenge in my corporate law career. In the eyes of my firm, I existed merely to improve their bottom line, and they really didn't care what I had to sacrifice to achieve that goal.

My perspective was antithetical: I was not willing to sacrifice for someone who did not return the favor. While I was pregnant with my second son, my health reached a critical point and I nearly died. Not one partner or manager from the firm came to see me, or even called. As I gazed at my newborn son, everything came crashing into clarity: my job, which had previously defined me, was no longer worth sacrificing my children, health or happiness for.

During my maternity leave, I contemplated the horror of returning to work. It felt like I was selling my soul. The next step was clear: I had to leave the "corporate" practice of law and start my own firm.

I set myself up in my own practice, but things didn't go exactly as I'd planned. I was still not finding the happiness and fulfillment my soul was longing for. More, I was plagued by many of the same challenges I struggled with in my old firm— like endless hours and a crazy workload—only now, I was now the face and name of the practice. The balance between work and my home life was still a struggle, and my "spiritually aligned" vision for my practice didn't pay the rent and bills, so I was back to taking whatever clients walked through the door and mopping up the inevitable messes.

I still craved spiritual connection. I still snuck away after the kids went to bed so my friend could read my cards or do some healing work on me. I was still reading every book on spirituality I could get my hands on.

And I still felt completely isolated.

I heard my calling to my work in the spiritual realm, and could see my path, but that judgmental inner voice was louder than ever. "What will your law clients think?" It taunted. "What is your mother going to say?" So I sneakily started a small coaching practice using an alias. It was fun, and I enjoyed a little success with it—but I was still hiding, and I still had *huge* fears and limiting beliefs around others' opinions of my choices.

While driving home one night from a class, I came to a stop light. That light seemed particularly long (or I may have sat through a few turns of it, I'm not sure. It was really late, and there were few others cars on the road). As I waited, I observed the true happiness, joy, and excitement I felt. I had spent the evening doing what I loved, talking to dead people and sharing their message with the living. I had provided healing, comfort and answers to people who were in despair and feeling helpless. I had helped them without anyone else losing or being injured by my work.

My answer had been so long before me, and I had been too scared to see and accept it, let alone say it out loud.

In that moment of clarity, I was able to put aside my ego and all the inner voices to truly enjoy the happiness that was pouring from me. I was completely aligned with my soul's purpose and the vibration of what I wanted to do.

Finally, I noticed the light turn green. The rest of my drive home may have taken twice the time it normally did, or it may have been much shorter. Lost in the euphoria of alignment, I had no concept of time.

Unfortunately, my joy was fleeting. The next day, I had to re-emerge as a lawyer. I woke up with a headache that left me seeing double and barely able to stand, but I had to be in court that morning, so I chugged down multiple cups of coffee and stumbled into the office. I prepped for my hearing at a snail's pace, and felt nauseous as I pulled into the parking lot outside the hearing office.

I tried to convince myself that it was the headache causing my queasiness, but I knew it was misalignment that was plaguing me. I felt like I was living a lie. I was physically present, but my thoughts were far, far away. As soon as the gavel dropped, I was out the door without even a word to my client.

This was *not* going to work. I could not let the expectations of others dictate my course and drag me back to the place I had been trapped for so long.

Later, as I sat on my sunny back porch and tried to melt away the drama and chaos of work, it became absolutely clear what my next right step was. The vision of what I had to do in order to save myself and my career—yes, both of them, because one could not exist without the other—played in my head like I was watching it on a movie screen. I had to stop hiding, start living authentically, and embrace what my soul was calling me to do.

That very night, I ditched the alias and bought my domain name—my real name—and started coaching and conducting readings publicly.

It took me a while to comfortably meld my two personas into one professional woman, let alone speak publicly about it, but I did it! I still run my own law practice, where I represent only people I feel aligned with, and take only the files I feel called to take. I also coach women who find themselves in the same rut I was in to find, and live in, aligned fulfillment. I can speak freely with clients from either role, about everything I do.

It feels tremendously aligned (if still absolutely frightening) to show up in the public eye as exactly the woman I am, and not what others think I should be. Yes, I still encounter closed-minded members of my community (both virtual and in-person) who find it necessary to share their opinions about what I "should" be doing with my education—but I have learned not to care about the opinions and judgments of others. As Dr. Wayne Dyer wrote, "What others think of me is really none of my business."

I feel like I am living the life of a superhero. I truly am Wonder Woman—and it's not just my Underoos talking! So many women long to be able to follow the path they know is theirs, but cannot ... yet. It is my responsibility to carry a torch for those women and show them the way.

REFLECTIONS

Is the voice that steers you your own, or is it the influence of society and all the voices in your past that have passed judgment on you?

_____

_____

_____

_____

What helps you hear your own voice—and how do you muster the courage to listen to it?

_____

_____

_____

_____

Do you think that "alignment" is something you do, something you live, or both?

_____

_____

_____

_____

LEADING BY EXAMPLE

Amanda Hinman

I was living as *appears-to-have-it-all-together Amanda*: engrossed as an involved mother of four, an impeccable wife, and an energetic fitness coach. The pattern of ignoring my inner voice was a consistent theme in my life. I teeter-tottered back and forth between grabbing a glass of wine or a piece of chocolate to unwind in the evening, and waking up the next morning filled with guilt over my lack of willpower.

I barked orders at my girls more often than I spoke with encouragement and love. I reacted to small everyday inconveniences as if they were major catastrophes. Rather than nurturing my family, I took it upon myself to manage them.

My dream-chasing oldest daughter's desires to make new recipes and leave trails wherever she went received disapproving looks. My energetic second daughter's need to walk around in clickity high-heeled shoes caused me to constantly ask her to change who she was. My inquisitive third daughter's continuous stream of questions received rushed responses and requests for her to be quiet. My stop-and-smell the roses fourth daughter's desire to finish coloring a picture and move at a snail's pace drew exasperated breaths and annoyed frowns.

The people I was supposed to love unconditionally possessed qualities that irritated, annoyed, and derailed my carefully planned agenda—one that was all about efficiency, perfection, and control.

I ignored my inner voice which craved time to recharge, just as much as my daughters and husband tuned out my requests to brush their teeth before school or skip the second beer with dinner. I felt powerless over my ability to be heard, to create time for myself and especially to be clear on how to feel happy and healthy. My resentment built.

The steady wave of negative emotions progressed for five years and came to a breaking point on one stormy afternoon in April. The weather outside the hospital room window mirrored my despair as I listened to the pediatric neurologist explain why my eight-year-old daughter needed seizure medication that included four pages of possible negative side effects. I felt nauseated. I couldn't comprehend how we were in this place. I glanced over to see my daughter's petite silhouette lying in the hospital bed; her body weakened in the aftermath of her fourth seizure. My stomach clenched in knots and my head swirled. I couldn't stand upright.

I had been unknowingly role-modeling for my daughter how to "do everything right" at the expense of listening to my body. I focused on others' perceptions, rather than my well-being. She followed my example when her anxious thoughts increased to the point of causing seizures.

The next four months were a roller-coaster. I lived like a jack-in-the-box alternating between feeling hopeful and then completely devastated as her seizures intensified. I sought out second opinions, made drastic changes to our family's diet, took her to a chiropractor, and a therapist. Every fiber of my being fought to rebuild her health.

However, my flurry of action didn't have the impact I'd hoped for. My daughter continued to have seizures, as many as ten to fifteen in a day. She took four different seizure medications. I no longer recognized my once-passionate and witty girl because she was now distant and lethargic due to the side effects from her many medications.

Finally, my exhaustion and powerlessness reached a threshold. I stopped fighting alone and allowed myself to surrender to help. I made a courageous decision to follow my heart and invest in a coach to get support for myself. This decision changed my life and my family's life for good.

The amazing thing was as I started carving out time for self-care I became energized. My passion for holistic health recharged, I discovered how to notice my emotions, nutrition, and communication. I eagerly learned the importance of balancing activity that felt good to my body with intentional downtime in my life. It was as if a small rose deep inside my heart was starting to open up one petal at a time. I began listening to my inner voice and trusting my intuition which provided clarity and confidence. The best part was experiencing the ripple effect it had on my family.

As I softened, I noticed my daughter shifting too. There were moments of laughter in our family again. Her seizures began to fade into the past. I felt optimistic that our life could be normal again.

I grew more deeply connected to my family. I learned to slow down and become curious. Instead of feeling irritated when my oldest daughter broke into hysterics after forgetting a field trip form for school, I asked why she was so upset and realized it was because she was worried about being perceived as irresponsible.

I could relate and empathize.

The journey to shift and prioritize self-care wasn't always easy. At first, I felt guilty taking time away from my family to work with a coach and carve space for my personal development and relaxation. One night at dinner, I explained through tears how exhausted and overwhelmed I was and how I needed help because I didn't want to continue dictating to the girls and giving the silent treatment to my husband. I had been the one to carry out all of the household work and this new approach meant I had to ask my family to take on things like meal preparation and laundry.

Along the way, I felt some sadness and second guessing as well. Previously, I was a person who was very involved in everything in my daughters' lives, from Parent Teacher Council President to gymnastics team parent volunteer. I was the mom who hosted weekly play dates and Halloween parties. Part of my journey to reconnect with myself meant letting some of these things go.

Each day offered another chance to focus on the positive aspects of my life and live in the present moment. Previously, I started my morning with a running to-do list in my head and would rattle off all the things the girls needed to do to get ready for school. The new routine of waking up twenty minutes earlier to journal about things I was grateful for took some getting used to. However, once I experienced how impactful it was in shifting my mindset and mood, I was hooked.

I committed to making this new way of living stick, so my family began to trust things weren't going to go back to what they had been before.

Almost a year after I had been staring out the hospital window at the rain, my daughter and I sat in the doctor's office. We listened to his response at my suggestion that we begin to wean her off medication. My motherly intuition was strong and understood she now lived differently. She had learned from my example to listen to what her body needed to heal and shift her emotions.

At that moment, I became aware of the different space I experienced because of the decision to invest in myself and get support ... a place of clarity and confidence.

I entered the discussion about my daughter's health as an equal rather than feeling powerless and uncertain. I recognized my insight in the form of motherly intuition and used this knowledge to collaborate with our doctor on my daughter's behalf. I felt simultaneously uplifted and completely at peace.

A sense of calm washed over both of us as we agreed on a time frame to wean off her medication.

My daughter's path, an enjoyable, steady momentum, gently guided her toward health. Ultimately, she discovered how to trust in her inner voice the same way I had learned to do. She has been medication-free and seizure-free for three years, and I am forever grateful to her for shining a spotlight on the cost of trying to live an inauthentic life. If it weren't for her challenge, I wouldn't understand that my frustration, overwhelm, and guilt as a mom was teaching my children to live the same way.

I believe life always provides opportunities to invest in, transform, and empower ourselves, and doing so is a gift to everyone we love. Now I live my passion helping other moms tune into their voice, create time for things they are passionate about, and discover clarity and confidence in supporting their families.

REFLECTIONS

How do you speak to your loved ones? Do your words resonate with encouragement and love?

_____

_____

_____

_____

How deeply do you trust your intuition when it comes to your own health and the health of your loved ones? How can you honor your inner knowing?

_____

_____

_____

_____

What do you think is the "cost of living an inauthentic life?"

_____

_____

_____

_____

SMASH IT ALL AND BUILD ANEW

Michelle Mercier

*M*y beautiful baby boy came into this world in 2016 with medical complications. The day after he was born, the doctor came in to discuss the fact that they had discovered issues with my baby's heart. A familiar feeling of panic crept into my body. Was this really happening? Hadn't we just spent the past two years getting his older brother's medical conditions under control?

I turned to my husband, and the only words I uttered were, "I don't know if my heart can take this again. It hurts so much."

We met immediately with a pediatric cardiologist. My sweet baby's medical team also grew to include an Ear, Nose, and Throat specialist because my son had an airway defect and a Gastroenterology team due to his severe acid reflux. I watched every day as my son struggled to breathe, sometimes turning blue in my arms. We spent endless hours at doctors' appointments, in emergency rooms, and hospitals.

I felt overwhelmed, exhausted, and petrified that I was failing as a parent. Every new mom of two worries about how to split herself between the needs of two children. That being said, no one prepared me for the roller coaster of emotions that accompanied having two sons with medical complications: competing medical appointments, the litany of doctors and treatments to keep straight, and the heartache of comforting two children while they underwent testing. Functioning was an uphill battle, but I pushed forward with the determination only a mother could possess. Giving up was never an option when it came to my children.

Life seemed to calm down around the third month of my little man's life. He wasn't completely out of the woods, but he was stable, thriving, and a plan was in place. Luckily, his brother was also stable. At that moment, our family collectively exhaled and prepared for my return to work.

I looked forward to work adding a sense of routine and normalcy back into our lives. Also, working was my way of avoiding the parts of my life that hurt. I had thrown myself into my job when my first son got sick. I worked sixty hour weeks, juggled doctors' appointments, and climbed the corporate ladder. This familiar, dysfunctional coping mechanism felt comfortable. Little did I know, the universe had a different plan.

It was a sunny morning in April when I received the call. I was laid off. I lost my ability to stand when I heard the news and began sobbing the minute the phone call ended. I texted my husband, who came home immediately. He understood that this was a game changer for me. The universe had thrown so much at our family—ripped the rug out from under us so many times—that he knew I was at my breaking point. He found me on our kitchen floor in the middle of a massive anxiety attack. That one phone call destroyed my coping mechanism and shattered me into a million pieces.

I'm not sure what finally snapped me out of that emotional place on the floor, but there is one thing I know for certain. There was a reason I fell to my knees during that phone call. That position is a place of prayer, surrender, and it's where true greatness begins. From my knees, I waved the white flag at the Universe and heard a small voice inside me whisper "It's time to shatter. Smash it all and build anew."

I took the advice to heart. I broke down and mourned a version of myself that was not coming back. The future was unclear, but I found solace in the fact that the rebuilding period was coming. Throughout this shattering, a small voice from within encouraged me to be still and reflect. I constantly heard the words, "Stop so you can hear yourself. You cannot outrun every thought and emotion inside of you."

I used this time to reflect on the past decade and the person I'd become. Growing up, I'd never wanted to work in the corporate sector. As an artist, I had dreams of spending my life creating and helping others. At some point, I decided that was not a "responsible" way to live so I compromised my creativity and stepped into a role that fit better with the standards in which I felt I "should" live. I climbed the corporate ladder and excelled at my job. I convinced myself that because I was extremely good at my work, I must be happy. Nothing could have been farther from the truth. I wasn't happy working sixty hours a week and it didn't fill my soul with joy. Instead, it made me numb, so I never had to face the emotional turmoil in my life. I wondered what other areas of my life weren't authentic. What other decisions had I made from a place of false happiness? Did I even know what made me happy?

My thoughts turned to a question that I'd been pondering for weeks. What would life look like if nothing stood in my way? I sat at my desk and wrote about a life without limitations and allowed myself to dream for the first time in years. I wrote down details of what my ideal personal and professional life would look like. I wove in creativity, abundance, and the space to hear myself think.

I wanted a life filled with positive energy, fun, and laughter! I wanted to be fully present with my family and not always feel rushed. I wanted to feel inspired by the work I did on a daily basis.

More than anything, I wanted to be truly happy and deeply satisfied by life.

These feelings inspired me to start my own company. I started by simply speaking my truth through blog posts, videos, and events. The most amazing thing happened. Women started reaching out to me to speak their truths. I received emotional and deeply personal confessions from people I had known for years. People thanked me for making them feel less alone in their situation. I was astonished by how many people were just waiting for someone to speak first.

The conversations were reminders that it was vastly important to speak truthfully about the struggles of life because we're all experiencing them. They may not have realized it, but speaking to these individuals brought me back to life and gave me the courage to keep moving forward. It also gave me a renewed appreciation of the never-ending resilience and strength that women possess.

My family was most positively impacted by my new life approach. I felt an overwhelming sense of joy watching the glow of my transformation shine on my family. I never realized how much my constant running had impacted them. Patience, meaningful conversations, and laughter replaced the rushed routines, hastened hugs, and missed bedtimes. My incredible husband told me on a regular basis how proud he was of me. During my rebuilding, his unconditional love, support, and respect taught me the true meaning of partnership. My oldest son started to show kindness and gratitude that took my breath away. He no longer had to compete with a high-pressure job for my attention, and it showed. Now, I make a point to spend dedicated time laughing, playing, and connecting with him.

As for my youngest son, I truly believe the universe sent him here to serve as the spark that ignited my change. Because of all this, I was given the gift of being truly present for every appointment, decision, and milestone of his first year. He needed me as much as I needed him during that period. His infectious smile lit me up throughout my rebuilding. His strength showed me just how strong I could be.

This entire journey helped me realize how close I came to waking up one day, looking around, and not seeing anything that represented my true self. I will always be grateful for that morning on the kitchen floor because, had I not chosen to shatter and wave the white flag at the universe, I would have missed out on so many amazing moments in life. I would never have gotten the chance to "smash it all and build anew."

REFLECTIONS

Michelle used her work to escape the stress and challenging emotions of the other parts of her life. What is your "escape"? Does it serve you, or are you using it as a crutch?

_____

_____

_____

_____

When was the last time you were brought to your knees? What did you learn in that moment?

_____

_____

_____

_____

What do you think would happen if you spoke your truth unconditionally?

_____

_____

_____

_____

BECOMING MYSELF

Robin Reid

*B*ankruptcy.

The multi-million dollar manufacturing business I had developed from nothing and nurtured for over twenty productive years was shuttered. I felt breathless, shriveled, and cold. I couldn't believe that it was over. Without my company's testament to my capabilities and worth, meaning drained out of my life. Who was I without the flourishing highway of commerce, without contributing to the greater community, without my connection to "normalcy?"

Then came the dream.

In my dream, I walked through sparse woods on a hill. Birdsong filled the soft spring air. An older woman slowly made her way through the trees, scanning the ground, stopping now and then to pick something from the grass and nestle it into the basket on her arm. Though I didn't know her, she felt familiar to me. As I approached, she looked up, and a broad smile spread across her face.

"I have been waiting for you, my dear." Her eyes danced, full of sparkle and promise. "My cabin is just ahead. Join me for a cup of tea. We must talk."

I followed her into the warm and cozy cabin full of herbs and candles. I felt ... at home.

In reality, I have not always felt at home.

Growing up as the oldest child of a Wisconsin farm family, practicality was the order of the day. There was no room for or understanding of esoteric ideas or spiritual exploration. However, there was never a time in my life when I did not "know" things, or understand instinctively why people did what they did. When I was little, I played at being an old lady healer who went around the countryside taking care of people and talking about God. Quite often, I had a deep understanding about life that ranged far beyond my years.

My family, however, was not amused by my enthusiastic proclamations and actively discouraged me from talking about "weird stuff." Ashamed and embarrassed, I tried to hide my knowing, and threw myself into helping others in more practical ways. I strove to become "normal."

Throughout my childhood and into my teens, I sought to please, to be dependable, to fit in. Often, I felt rebuffed, misunderstood, and ignored, sensing that there was something wrong, either with me or with what I was doing. These were lonely and painful years as I struggled with anxiety, frustration, and depression.

I felt a strong yearning inside me to hear and understand Spirit, and knew I would eventually find a way to express it. I clung to my unshakable childhood belief that the way would appear— that I would eventually become the healer I was supposed to be, and do the work I was destined to do.

After college, I was drawn to business. Dealing with products gave me the smokescreen behind which I could hide my delight in providing spiritual healing and guidance. Proving that I was capable and efficient gave me solace for the anguish I felt at being different. I worked hard and had considerable success on many levels, secretly following my intuition in making business decisions. I eventually established a thriving manufacturing business, which allowed me to raise a family, employ hundreds of local people, and make a positive impact in my community.

Through it all, I continued to nurture my growing need for

a deeper understanding of my spiritual gifts. I explored a wide variety of personal development and consciousness-raising courses, including years of study in energy healing with one of the world's best-known practitioners. Study of the esoteric arts was my passion and longing, and formal coaching both validated and deepened my belief that I was on the right path. My business blossomed. It seemed the further out I took my studies of healing arts, the better my personal life became.

It was about this time that I visited Glastonbury in England and climbed the Tor, where there are remains of an old church tower. There, I had an experience of passing into another dimension, as though the fabric between the past and the present had been breached, and I heard voices clearly telling me that, from now on, I should expect guides to appear to me and assist me in my life journey. The adventure left me intensely energized and a bit disoriented. It took only days for the sense of nausea and "unreality" to subside, but years to fine-tune my confidence and ability to communicate to others the information I was given.

Then everything came tumbling down. Suddenly, the company was insolvent, a result of trust misplaced and clues misread. I was devastated and wanted to crawl away to hide forever. The Universe had just given me another step closer to my real self, although it didn't appear that way at the time. I heard the guidance to offer my gifts of counsel and Spirit, but I was terrified to show who I truly was in a seemingly hostile world.

I took a series of unsatisfactory jobs working for other people until I finally landed a job with a large non-profit organization. I joyfully crafted inspirational stories of hope and philanthropy, promoting the extraordinary work of that great organization. But leadership models changed and skills other than mine were needed; I suddenly found I was bone-tired of working so hard to be whom someone else wanted me to be.

This time I listened to what the Universe was saying, "There is no place left in this outer world for you. It's time to do your work from the inner world." Unknown to me, a good friend recommended me for an opening as a medium at a small spiritualist camp close to my home. They called and invited me to interview, I was immediately accepted, and starting work there on my birthday of that year.

As I drove to the camp, I felt scared, but I had a clear realization that I could never go back to "regular business," and that this—my birthday—was the birth of my new way, my real self. It was an emotionally overwhelming recognition that this new venture was what I had been moving towards all my life.

The camp was on a wooded hill. Warm sun filtered through the trees as I walked to my little cabin where I set out herbs and candles to greet my first clients. It became clear that the events in my dream had come full circle. Finally, the knowledge I had as a child that I would be a healer, and my vision of the woman in the woods, had come true.

I'd suppressed my inner calling for almost my entire life, but the Universe finally determined that my internal experience was too powerful to deny. By fulfilling my external experience, I'd denied my true self, even though I always knew it was there, and even though every aspect of my external life had prepared me in many different ways for this destination at which I now found myself.

I no longer wonder what's missing in my life. I feel authentic. I'm not afraid that people will "find me out," I'm no longer hiding the nature of who I am and what I do, and I no longer make excuses for my beliefs or views. The freedom this change has afforded me is immeasurable.

Growing my coaching and healing practice has been a relatively easy process. Other people who have also been hiding have found me and are grateful to me as a role model and guide for expressing and exploring their inner lives. I'm frequently invited to speak publicly on my favorite subjects—energy healing, intuition, other dimensions, and angels—and to take spiritual leadership roles.

To my surprise, my family and friends have heartily supported this shift in my identity and direction. But what is most gratifying is that I feel like I can do this for the rest of my life. I'm excited by the prospect of my work and by the loving kindness it generates. When I'm with clients, my energy increases and expands rather than depleting, and I relish every moment that the inner child who never lost sight of her goal has been vindicated in her belief. I have become myself.

I am ... home.

REFLECTIONS

Have you ever changed or hidden your true self in order to "fit in" with others? How did it feel?

_____

_____

_____

_____

Robin wasn't ready to list her inner calling until she had exhausted her options in the "outer world." What would make it possible for you to listen to your inner voice above all else?

_____

_____

_____

_____

What was your connection to Spirit as a child? What aspects of that relationship can you bring forward to serve you now?

_____

_____

_____

_____

CHAPTER

Four

THE COURAGE TO HEAL

SACRED HEALING

Cindy Hively

*T*he day I woke up from being diagnosed with a serious chronic illness was frightening—but at the same time, a relief.

By the time I was diagnosed, my body and my sense of being were completely gone. The chronic pain had been excruciating. The emergency room visits seemed endless. I wasn't existing by choice as I lay day after day in bed with the curtains closed. My identity was stripped from me, and the job I loved was gone. I was anxious all the time, food made me feel sick, and I couldn't walk without a cane or help from my husband. I needed help with my bath and just about every other activity I had taken for granted all my life. I wanted to be left alone.

How could my own body betray me like this? I wasn't a mother, wife, daughter, sister, or employee; I was a shell where pain and darkness resided. What I didn't know then was that I would awaken to life six months after my diagnosis.

On a cold, snowy January day in 2010, I opened my blinds slightly to look out at the weather: at that moment, the miracle and magic I needed in my life appeared. As I watched beautiful snowflakes coming down, I was mesmerized by their beauty, purity, and uniqueness. Then, a question from within me surfaced: "Why did my life move to this cruel dark place and make me different?"

My heart cracked open, and I knew I had a choice to make. I could keep lying in that bed for the rest of my life, or I could get up and start figuring life out one step at a time. And that is exactly what I did. I never expected what was coming next. If I had known, I would have probably pulled the blinds shut again.

I spent the next few years coping with pain. I still struggled most days, but those struggles only made me more rebellious. It was the enlightened rebelliousness of awakened consciousness that formed an unshakable foundation to healing. I refused to let my body take control of me: I was in charge.

I had been so busy from the time I graduated from college in 1987 up until my diagnosis that I didn't see the beauty in life: the changes, the brilliance, and all the amazing gifts from the Divine creator. Suddenly, I started to see beauty in everything. The most healing times were in the beauty of darkness: I connected to my sanctuary within and released. Seeing Beauty in my everyday life flowed from the time I opened my eyes until I fell asleep at night. I found nature to be overflowing with beauty as I took my walks or even did the dishes. Yes: I washed and felt the texture of the plates, and the flowing warm water on my hands soothed me.

I started connecting with my very soul: I was changing. My belief system was different, my values were different, and supportive people and opportunities started showing up in my life. I knew something magical was taking place. I didn't know what, why, or when, but I felt the energy running through me. During this time, I wrote in my blog about my experiences and healing. By speaking, writing, and being so true to myself, my life shifted dramatically. I knew that if I wanted to keep awakening to my true nature, I could never allow myself to stumble. I had to be true to myself. I was incredibly present, and it took courage to continue on this path. It required innocence, the discovery of new ways of living, and the release of all the fixed beliefs and concepts from years of conditioning. Living in courage for me was living in nonresistance.

During this time, I was also very connected to one word that kept popping up: "Goddess."

I started researching The Goddess and living from the Divine Feminine. I studied the keepers of the secret and ancient healing modalities. I started following the lunar phases in my life, and realized this was who I always have been. As a child, I loved night: looking up at the moon and stars, creating my own celestial dots. I loved digging in the dirt and planting with my grandmas, and putting food on the table fresh out of the earth. The smell of fresh rosemary made me smile. Fresh dill made my cheeks pucker. If I had a tummy ache, my grandma would put a few ingredients together and tell me to drink up. During the summer, I begged my parents to take me a few states away to stay with my grandmas. Thank goodness, they both lived in the same town.

As I studied and started taking course work in essential oils, herbal remedies, and the path of the Goddess, I continued to heal. My mind, body, and Spirit were connecting and working together. I would get to a certain point during this time, however, and then shut down a few days at a time. My biggest fear was that I would lose my way back to Her.

On a beautiful summer night just a few years ago, I looked up at the sky and asked God to show me what I was missing. Why was it difficult for me to truly call myself a Goddess, a Healer, and Woman who believed we are created in a Divine Spiritual way? Within thirty seconds, the answer I was so fearful of looking at stared me straight in the face. I couldn't move a muscle; I was so frightened I was afraid of my own breath. The answer was this: I wasn't brought up to believe in the way that was in alignment with my nature. I was brought up in a stoic Baptist home and went to Bible College. How on Earth was I going to live in the way I wanted to, the way I was so connected with?

In all my years of growing up in the church, I can never remember the Goddess being talked about. I remember very little of biblical women being discussed at all. I don't believe that the Divine chooses only Man; due to society and hundreds of years of women being conditioned, generation after generation, this is simply where we are now.

I started asking myself, my mentors, and my dear friends lots of questions, and I received support and good information. I also realized how much value came from having a minor in Religion from college. I remember sharing my website with my mom. She asked, "What is a Goddess?" She sounded worried. I asked her if she believed we are created as Divine beings from God. She did believe all is divinely created. I explained that all women are divinely created, and are Goddesses.

I very cautiously started out on my own transformational journey again, but this time I was stronger, more courageous, and determined to let Spirit co-create with me. I was a Goddess on a mission to continue to heal, and to invite other Women to share my journey with me. This was my calling: this is what was being asked of me, and what I continue to do today.

When I finally came to the place where I realized I didn't need my family or friends' validation, or any belief system's approval, I knew that the only thing stopping me was myself. It has been a little over two years since my life has fully unfolded in this way, and I continue to find courage in new ways of being. I keep creating new vortexes in my life. Working with nature, the elements, and all of creation is pure magic to me. It is sometimes uncomfortable, but I know I need to walk through the experience to find the clarity I need. As I create more ways of being, I heal—and so do my clients. That is the badge of courage that makes me wake up with purpose every morning. Knowing in each moment I create what happens next in my life—that I get to choose—is a beautiful, divine gift.

Each morning in my daily life, I allow my mystic nature to consciously direct me: I move into what I need most to gain clarity, and to discover more spaciousness, healing, and wisdom. Lurking in the shadows of my interior, I must continue to release and shed my older identity. It brings me to more fear than any other tool or strategy as I live as a Goddess and now Priestess. Letting go of what I believed about myself for over forty-five years is not easy. Sometimes, I look back at my illness and realize it was (and is) much easier to be ill than to peel back the layers as I continue to dig deeper. As I light my inner flame and walk through the darkness and fire, I come out anew. I may walk with fear as I choose this path, but I always rise more courageousness and inspired, and with greater harmony and healing.

I don't know what has been my most courageous moment. I truly believe that the last several years have required many courageous moments as I form, and live from, a new place of identity. I am so much stronger for living in my truth and through love and compassion. I have indeed come home to my sacredness of life.

REFLECTIONS

Has something brought you to your knees for healing—for example, an illness or life difficulty?

_____

_____

_____

_____

How do you define the word "Goddess"?

_____

_____

_____

_____

How do you connect with your Divine Feminine? What value does this practice bring to your daily life?

_____

_____

_____

_____

THE COURAGE TO LET GO

Felicia D'Haiti

*M*y husband and I sat by my brother's hospital bed for nearly twelve hours, making sure that he looked comfortable. It had suddenly become a ritual, and we performed it each day—sitting, waiting, watching and listening. On most days, I was there by myself, talking to my unconscious brother, the nurses, or some visitors. Visitors came on and off throughout the days. Many were cousins and friends whom I had not seen in quite some time. The nurses were kind and helpful, but this was certainly not how I pictured spending time with my brother, Joseph.

This day was different, though. My husband offered to come with me because neither of us was going to work that day. We drove to the hospital in the morning and sat through the entire day, only taking breaks to get coffee or a bite to eat. We'd been there nearly all day when one of Joe's favorite cousins came to visit. When she left, we prepared to leave as well. Even though I was tired, I had been waiting for the nurses to change shifts so that I could meet the night shift nurse and get an update on my brother. All day I had been listening to the sounds of his shallow breath and the typical hospital background noises, wondering why events were unfolding this way.

Finally, the night nurse came to check on him. She came, took his temperature, and tried to take his blood pressure. The machine appeared to be going crazy. The numbers kept spiking and dropping rapidly. Just as quickly as she came, she was gone again to get another machine. In that moment, silence enveloped the room. I felt as if the world had stopped spinning: I suddenly realized that my brother had transitioned. At that moment, I felt like my own heart had stopped beating. My husband went to call a nurse in to check him. Several nurses came and confirmed that he had died. I was simultaneously crushed and relieved. I was glad for him that he was no longer in discomfort or pain, but I was terribly upset for myself for so many reasons.

Growing up, I always felt a sense of responsibility for my baby brother. Not only because there were just the two of us, but also because he had Down Syndrome. I've been quite protective of him. My parents were older than most of my friends' parents; they were nearly forty years old when they married. I'm uncertain at what age I was made aware that my parents had planned for my brother's care after they transitioned. I'm not sure at what age I was aware that my brother was different. But at some point, I took on the future responsibility of becoming caregiver when my parents were gone. I became especially aware of this when my mother died unexpectedly twelve years ago.

I was quite certain that I would be taking care of Joe into his old age. My husband also accepted this future responsibility when we got married. Each of our homes has had a bedroom that we called his, a place for him to live when he moved out of my parents' home. I was so very sure that life would unfold this way that this future was part of my identity.

We are still not certain exactly what happened to cause the decline in my brother's health. We noticed he had been losing weight over some months, but it wasn't a rapid weight loss, and he said he was fine. In October, though, he was taken to the hospital because he was having trouble swallowing. After some examinations and a medical procedure, he was sent home. He did not improve. The last Friday in October, my dad asked if my husband and I would take Joe to the hospital emergency room for more testing and to find out why he was still unable to eat.

When we arrived at my dad's home, my brother took quite some time to recognize me. We helped him to the car and took him to the hospital. Once there, we waited hours for him to be checked in and evaluated. We reassured him that everything would be fine and that he'd be home in time for Dad's birthday on October 31. We left him after he had been checked in and settled into his room by the nurses. It never occurred to me that this would be the last time I would have a conversation with him.

That weekend in the hospital, Joe had a seizure and never regained consciousness. We waited for more tests, doctors, meetings, care team conferences, and more—only to be told that his brain functions were severely damaged and there was little chance of recovery. Two weeks after we checked him in to the hospital, I sat in a meeting with a counselor, a doctor, a social worker, my husband, and my father. I heard my brother's prognosis, and the hospital staff gave us a copy of my brother's health care directive. It included his signed wishes: he did not want to be on life support.

It may seem that this should have made everything easier. We knew what his wishes were even though he could not tell us what he wanted. And while it was freeing in some ways, it challenged me even more to let go of him and to let go of the part of myself, my identity, and the future I had laid out for both of us. Within days of the joint family decision to remove life support, my taking care of my brother transformed in ways I had never imagined it would. My care became my bedside vigil, my prayers, and eventually, my planning of his funeral with my father.

In the week after my brother's death, two family members approached me, recalling recent conversations with my brother during which he told them he was ready to die because he missed our mom. Here were some messages that he was ready to let go.

But was I? I'm not quite sure how I made it through the weeks leading up to and including my brother's funeral just like I'm still not quite sure how I survived and became healthy again after my battle with cancer a year ago.

When everything was over, I had time to reflect on what happened and on people's comments to me. Some referred to my courage: I had difficulty associating the word courage with anything that I'd done. Through my cancer and the events surrounding my brother's death, I felt as if I did what I had to do. I looked up the word courage in the dictionary, and found that one of the meanings is "strength in the face of pain or grief." I'd never thought of courage in that way.

When I think back to how I made it through, how I "did what I had to do," I am reminded of the daily practices that help me get through challenging times. When I was first diagnosed with cancer, all the details, bad news, and thoughts faded into the background as I focused on being fully healthy, knowing that I would have to let go of parts of myself in the process. The events leading up to and including the loss of my brother were quite similar in many ways. I found myself more focused on treasuring every moment, making time to sit and reflect, and looking forward to allowing the best outcome for all involved.

My courage, though I still do not completely claim it, comes from trusting that the Universe will allow what is best for all in the end. It comes everyday in looking past the pain that my brother's absence has created to knowing that this is what he wanted. It comes from accepting what is placed before me to deal with, knowing that there is a resolution for every situation. My unrealized courage has come out of the circumstances of my journey to help me along the way in being able to let go when it is time and to be at peace with my path.

REFLECTIONS

What are the daily practices that help you get through challenging times?

_____

_____

_____

_____

Was there a time in your life when the most loving thing to do was to let go? What did you learn from that experience?

_____

_____

_____

_____

Is there a part of your identity that is wrapped up in caring for someone else? What does that relationship have to teach you?

_____

_____

_____

_____

HOLDING THE VISION

Mal Duane

O n September 9, 2008, I was sitting in a client's very formal dining room, presenting a plan to sell their home. Suddenly, I broke into a massive cold sweat. There were beads of perspiration all over my face. An excruciating, stabbing pain hit me just above my navel. My hands started to tremble.

My clients immediately noticed how ill I was feeling—my face was drained of color. They kindly offered me a glass of water, but I couldn't pick it up. I knew I needed to leave immediately and try to get home. I grabbed my briefcase and stumbled to my car. I wasn't sure I could drive at first, but I pushed myself with every ounce of strength I could muster. My hands turned sheet white as I gripped the wheel.

I pulled into the driveway of my home and leaned on the horn. I called my then-husband's cellphone, and told him he needed to come outside and get me out of the car. He ran out of the house and opened my car door. He was a doctor; I could tell by the look on his face that I did not look well.

Several phone calls later, we were on our way to the emergency room of the hospital where my primacy physician would meet us. The suspected prognosis was acute appendicitis.

Waiting to be admitted, I felt like I was going to die on the gurney. I was getting fuzzy and dizzy from the pain, and nausea was coming on fast.

After two MRIs, multiple x-rays, extensive blood work, and

a thorough exam, I was wheeled down to an operating room for emergency surgery. I have never been so grateful to get somewhere before. Soon, the pain would stop—or so I thought.

That was the beginning of an eighteen-month journey that became the biggest test of faith in my life.

The surgeon came to see me the next day and explained that I had an appendix that was ready to burst. He found quite a mess when he opened me up. He said I showed signs of long-term illness, and asked me how I had been for the past several months. I had felt a little off, and had some digestive issues, but no serious pain or illness. I had discussed the digestion with my primary doctor several times looking for remedies.

Three days later, I was released and given the usual post-op instructions: bed rest and go easy. I followed them. I worked a few hours a day from home, took antibiotics, and rested.

Exactly fourteen days later, I woke up and could not get out of bed. I had no appetite. By the end of the day I was in such extreme pain that my husband sent a limousine to take me back to the hospital. He met me at the emergency room. This attack was as severe as the first one—maybe even worse.

Very quickly, the doctors decided to operate. Another MRI showed a reoccurrence of massive infection as a result of the previous surgery. It would need to be reopened and left open after it was cleansed. This time I was so sick that when I left the hospital I needed a nurse to come twice daily to the house to medicate me and clean the fist-sized hole in my side.

It took nearly a month to get back on my feet. Six weeks out from the original surgery, the doctors had me come in for a consult. They told me they saw an enlargement to the duct of the pancreas, usually an indication of a tumor. I barely heard their words. We scheduled another round of MRIs with contrast so they could clarify their suspicions. The head of the pancreatic cancer department was reassuring me that early in the game, we had options. All I could hear was the word cancer.

Before the test, I meditated for two hours and then took the sedative they prescribed. I brought headphones and listened to Buddhist chanting right up until I went into the tube. The machine made its usual deafening sledgehammer noise, but I ignored it by chanting. I wore an eye mask. (If I had opened my eyes inside the tube, I would have had a massive anxiety attack.)

Instead of seeing pitch black behind my eyelids, I saw beautiful light, all the colors of rainbows. How could that be? I had absolutely no sense of fear about what was happening around me. My own thoughts were drowning out the fears from the C-word. While in that tube, I *knew* I was going to survive.

This was the beginning of my own path: I would not be consumed by the threat of pancreatic cancer, and would never lose faith that I would be well.

However, over the next several months my health declined. How could this be? More tests were ordered. I was hospitalized again. There were no answers: the dark cloud of a pancreatic tumor still hung over my head. I knew I couldn't give up. I just had to keep my faith and look for alternative measures to help me.

I would sit quietly and close my eyes and see only wellness in my future. I started making a list of all the things I could do to help with my health. I decided to get more aggressive with my own recovery and engaged in Reiki treatments and acupuncture. I maintained a daily meditation practice of an hour, followed by thirty minutes of journaling to reframe any fearful ideas that might pop into my head.

Here is one of the messages I received on April 17, 2009:

> *You need to remember that God is always with you. Your energy will be restored. Just keep faith. You are not alone when you do not feel well. Do not put any energy into something that does not serve you. You*

*are a faithful student and I have great plans for you.
I know you may not see this now. Plant your seeds
faithfully and watch them grow. Watch where you
put your attention and you will reclaim your healthy
balance.*

I knew only one thing as I splashed in the rough seas of potentially terminal illness: keep swimming, and you will get to the other side.

Every day, I got divine messages through my meditation assuring me that I would be well. I was told I had work to do; I would help many women living in fear. I must show them how I stayed strong when confronted with great challenges.

The more I embraced the idea of serving and helping women, the healthier I became. My primary focus was not on my illness, but on what I could do to help others.

The acupuncture treatments had an enormous impact on all the inflammation in my organs and body. It was a slow but steady process; I felt a little better after each treatment. After twelve months, I was symptom-free. In total, eighteen months had passed since the appendicitis. And for the first time, I really felt well.

I was scheduled for another dreaded MRI: this would determine a plan for surgery and possible treatment. I engaged in the most powerful conversation I have ever had while in my dressing cubicle. I said, "God if you want me to do the work with these women, I need to be well."

The next day I got the call from my primary doctor. He started the conversation almost apologetically—he had no medical explanation for me. I already knew in my heart what was coming next. The enlargement of the duct was gone. He said, "It doesn't make sense medically, but let's be happy."

I was happy. I also had my own answers. I had held an unwavering faith in my ability to get better, and I never once let go of it. I started to share a little about my meditation and acupuncture with him, but I could sense it wasn't a conversation he was ready for.

After that, I jumped onto my path. I knew what I needed to do. There was a book that needed to be birthed from all the lessons I had learned. I wrote my first book, *Alpha Chick*, and released it as a Valentine's Day gift to women on February 14, 2012.

That was the beginning for me. Now, I have coauthored three more best-sellers, and am now in this book. I have earned three coaching certifications, done over 250 interviews, and created two online groups with thousands of women as members.

I am here, I am alive, and I am so happy to be able to serve all the women who need to hear this message: *Believe in Yourself.* Your beliefs can create unstoppable courage when you need it most. My beliefs helped me heal from the scariest medical prognosis you can get. My medical team may not have an explanation, but I do.

Thank you, God, for taking care of me.

REFLECTIONS

Has there ever been a time you should've felt afraid, but chose to believe in your own strength instead? What was the outcome of that choice?

_____

_____

_____

_____

What tools do you use when you need to re-frame fearful thoughts? What tools would you like to start using?

_____

_____

_____

_____

How can you create a daily ritual that helps you practice and refine your fear-reducing tools?

_____

_____

_____

_____

EVERYTHING HAPPENS FOR A REASON

Tarah Abram

I sat silently in the doctor's office, the words from her mouth replaying in my head: "Abnormal ... cervical cancer." Tears flooded my eyes as I wondered about the impact on my husband and our three children. Having just come out of a two-year unplanned renovation (thanks, Mother Nature), I already felt tired and exhausted, my energy drained.

I *had* been feeling off, and it had been a long time since I'd had a check-up. Having been diagnosed with endometriosis, an underactive thyroid, and polycystic ovary syndrome (PCOS) at a young age, I knew something inside my body didn't feel quite right, so I scheduled a check-up. I had also noticed some unusual changes with my body.

Embarrassed by my tears, I quickly caught myself, wiped them away, and thought, "It could be worse. It's going to be fine." The gynecologist walked me down the hallway to visit my family doctor. I thought we were going to talk about getting a plan together; instead, we discussed another one of my test results.

My doctor, normally a jolly man who had a friendly demeanor and told jokes to my kids, looked somber. "Tarah, the mole biopsy came back abnormal." He showed me the report with the words "severe malignant melanoma" highlighted.

I felt overwhelmed, shocked to silence. A voice in my head said, "Just breathe, Tarah. It will be fine. You can figure this out. Stay calm." My face felt flushed, as though I had rosy cheeks. Heat washed over my body as my heart pounded.

I left the office, emotionally frozen. I saw my husband. How would I tell him the news? I knew if I remained confident and strong, he could, too. I needed his strength, not sadness. So I told him my health issues were just a hiccup. As we drove home, we both sat in silence. He held my hand tightly, and I just concentrated on breathing.

When we got home, my mom called. When I told her the news, we cried together. I spent that night pacing back and forth, crying, and stopping to reassure myself that all of this happened for a reason. "Tarah, everything will be okay."

I awoke the next day, puffy-eyed, and determined to make a plan. I called my dear friend, an acupuncturist, a woman of wisdom in ancient healing modalities. I shared with her my results, and we devised an action plan to move forward. Something inside me knew I would heal. I just had to figure out how. My friend encouraged me to see a highly recommended integrative doctor. I was grateful that an appointment was available before our imminent family vacation, the timing of which couldn't have been more perfect. I needed the rest and relaxation.

Despite not knowing what to expect from this doctor, I remained hopeful and open. On the day of my appointment, I nervously entered the room.

He reviewed all of my test results and asked what seemed like a million questions. Then he said, "I don't just fix a problem. I heal the body as a whole." He handed me a stack of books to read.

I switched gears from studying interior design, a true passion of mine, and instead began to read the books and watch as many documentaries as my brain could absorb. My feelings see-sawed between frustration and acceptance. But I was determined not to miss a future with my kids, especially after all the effort to bring them into the world with endometriosis and PCOS. Having anything other than a positive ending didn't seem fair, and I knew there had to be a bigger purpose for why this was happening.

For the first time in my life, I did what felt right to me despite what anyone thought. I walked every day to ground myself with mother earth. I thought only positive thoughts. I refuse to attach myself to an outcome or assume a result. I started a daily practice of gratitude. I refused to attach myself to the outcome or assume a result. I started a daily practice of gratitude. I had many things to be grateful for, and that was where I put my focus.

Based on my research, I began to juice vegetables, which turned out to be something I loved! I explored different combinations. Each sip I took felt like it was nourishing and healing my body. I loved to cook and create, so I saw this as an opportunity to learn how to make changes and find different ways of combining things. I taught my kids what I was learning. We adjusted our diets and mindset so they could grow up with knowledge of how to prevent themselves from experiencing this type of scare. Despite juicing being new to me, all of it just made sense. Just looking at my kids, their smiles, hugs, and laughter gave me reassurance.

Our vacation came, and I felt so grateful to be surrounded by the sunshine, ocean, and sacred family time. We had a life to live, dreams to follow, and memories to create. We came to this earth and chose each other, and there was so much love I couldn't imagine missing it.

After vacation ended, I continued to make lifestyle changes and invest my time into learning. As the months passed, waiting for the next steps seemed to take forever. My biopsy went to several pathologists and they advised me that surgery was necessary. I was told to prepare for the possibility that cancer may have spread to my lymph nodes. I knew that this wasn't positive news, but I still believed in the path I had chosen and reassured myself that it would all work out.

On the day I turned thirty-five, I went to the doctor's office to find out the biopsy results from where they had removed the mole from my breast. Waiting for the results felt like it took an eternity, but I remained calm, feeling that all the steps I had taken would ensure my health and longevity. When the doctor came in the room he looked on his computer to read the results, I felt chills all over my body. I was focused on breathing as slowly and deeply as I could.

His eyes opened wide, and he said, "Tarah! Congratulations. This seems unbelievable, but there isn't even a trace of one abnormal cell." He congratulated me several more times.

My brain froze, and I couldn't get out what I wanted to say, so I just smiled and said, "Thank you." It's a funny thing, but in some strange way, I already knew that's what he was going to say. I chose to follow my heart, and that is what got me well.

For many years I had given up my power and followed the guidance of others. This time was different. I chose to tackle my health challenges my way despite what anyone else thought. I didn't care if they agreed or not. Stepping into my power resulted in a positive outcome. These behaviors were new to me, as a lifelong people pleaser who attempted to make everyone else happy even if it made me miserable. I learned I couldn't help others if I didn't follow my truth.

This experience did happen for a reason. It happened so that I could understand the value of trusting in myself, making a choice, and following through with it no matter what the outcome. The knowledge I gained was invaluable, and the opportunity to teach my kids at a young age to live in tune with nature was something that might have been missed had I not been able to own and follow through with my choices. Since then I've continued to follow what feels right to me, belief in myself no matter what I wish to do. I realized that I was only disappointing myself when I didn't do what I wanted.

Now that I own my power and follow my heart, I have learned to guide my path, and the opportunities that have opened up for me are things I couldn't have dreamed of. This experience has reassured me everything really does happen for a reason, regardless if it takes a while to understand why. I know that as long as I listen to my intuition and do what feels right for me, I can't make a wrong choice.

REFLECTIONS

How do you cope when you receive shocking or unexpected news?

_____

_____

_____

_____

Where in your own life has focused positivity resulted in beyond-expected outcomes?

_____

_____

_____

_____

Do you believe that everything happens for a reason? Why or why not?

_____

_____

_____

_____

THE SIMPLE CHOICE THAT CHANGED MY LIFE

Katt Tozier

*H*ave you ever made an in-the-moment choice that ended up creating major change?

On New Year's Eve 2013, I made such a choice and, at the time, it seemed like a small decision. It turned out to be the first step in the right direction—the step that put me firmly on the path to the healing that I'd been seeking for decades.

I refer to 2013 as "The Year from Hell," as it was the year my whole life collapsed. By the eve of 2014, I was living alone in a small cabin in the woods with my dog a couple of miles down a dead-end dirt road.

For decades, I had been trying to hold everything together through worry and rigid control, and the events early that year finally broke me. Then, in a period of ten weeks, I discovered my husband's affair, we separated, he was hospitalized, my mother was hospitalized, my youngest child moved out, we sold our home, and my mother died.

That summer, I moved through my days in a fog of grief, anger, and regret, an empty shell. Chronic muscle and joint pain plagued me. Thyroid and adrenal issues left me exhausted. Frequent heart palpitations, anxiety, and panic attacks kept me from eating or sleeping well. I spent most of my time navigating turbulent emotions. By August of that year, I'd moved to the cabin to try to heal ... and I found out eighteen days later that my beloved dog, Maverick, had terminal kidney cancer.

I was completely shattered, and I was furious.

I spent weeks railing at the Universe, at God, at the angels, at anyone listening. What had I done that was so awful that everything was being taken away from me?

My life, up to that time, had been a long series of challenges: a violent childhood, multiple failed relationships with alcoholic men, chronic anxiety and pain, digestive and gynecological issues. Through it all, I tried my best to be a good mother to my four children.

I was done; I was sick of life, sick of living, sick of all the pain.

Then came the day I was out in the woods walking the trail with Maverick. To this day, I don't know what made me stop—it could only have been Divine intervention. Suddenly, I came out of the haze I'd been living in for months and I asked myself, "Is this how you want this gentle dog's last days to be? With you angry, anxious, and disconnected from life?"

And the answer was, no, I didn't. That day, I made a commitment to make whatever time Mav had left on this earth as peaceful and healthful as possible.

What started out as something I did for my dog became the start of healing for me. I'm a nurturer and caregiver by nature, so it was much easier for me to choose to help him than to choose to help myself.

I began to put all the practical things I knew back into place: nutrition, yoga, meditation, herbs and essential oils, hydration, and good sleep. These were the tools I'd used in the past to maintain some semblance of wellness amidst the chaos, but there was a problem: in the past, I'd used them to try to rigidly control my physical, mental, and emotional environments. I had missed a critical element: a spiritual connection.

I was raised in a typically patriarchal religion that had doctrines about "right and wrong"—in particular with regard to acceptable roles and behaviors for women. I'd long ago disconnected from any spiritual practice, with one notable exception: I've always talked with the angels and asked for their protection, especially for my children and grandchildren.

As the weeks unfolded, I discovered a local metaphysical shop that had a thriving spiritual community, and I was magnetized to it. I went there at every opportunity, formed relationships, and participated in classes and events.

On Samhain (October 31), I set an intention to allow the turning of the Wheel of the Year to bring in the energy of a new beginning for me. I incorporated a number of spiritual practices into my holistic wellness routine. I purposefully invoked my healing power, in particular through working with emotional energy and releasing all of the negative thoughts and emotions that weighed me down.

The lighter I became, the more I recognized the need to intentionally choose what I wanted to bring into my life. I realized I wasn't sure where to start; I'd lived my whole life reacting to the things around me, especially trying to do whatever was necessary to prevent a man's anger from escalating.

I chose a starting point. I knew what I didn't want in my life ever again, and that knowledge began to point the way to what I did want to bring into my life. I began to understand I actually had the power—and the right—to pick and choose.

New Year's Eve was a work day for me. I put in my ordinary eight hours as a quality control specialist reviewing medical transcription reports. Then, I grabbed some Chinese takeout—including a pint of pork strips for Maverick—and sat down on the floor in front of the coffee table to eat. I had a candle burning and some incense lit, and my favorite Steven Halpern CD playing. As I ate the food and fed Mav his pork strips, I was in a semi-meditative state, just pondering the turning of the calendar into a new year, and finally being done with a year that had held so much pain.

I began to think about new beginnings, about opportunity. In the weeks since Samhain, I had taken a number of baby steps toward healing, yet much of me was still tied up in anxiety, fear, and doubt. That night, I began to consider what might happen if I simply adopted an attitude of optimism and openness, a willingness to trust and allow, trusting myself and trusting the Divine. I immediately realized it sure couldn't get any worse!

On the spur of the moment, I created a small ritual, set my intention to move into 2014 with an attitude of optimism, openness, and opportunity, and released it all to the Universe.

Within just a few weeks, a series of synchronicities, and a couple of miraculous events, occurred that led me to an unexpected invitation (from a complete stranger) to move to a large organic farm. At the time, I wasn't considering moving and, in fact, was only six months into a two-year lease on the cabin. There was something about that invitation, though. I couldn't stop thinking about it. What my mind thought impossible, my heart knew was right. I ended up checking out the farm, and then I really knew it was meant to be.

My head still said it couldn't be done: I'd lose a fifteen hundred dollar security deposit if I moved and, at the time, that was a lot of money to lose. Then, out of nowhere, the cabin landlord advised me that Maine law dictated that he had to test the property for radon. The completed test results indicated dangerous levels in the cabin. Landlord-Tenant law stated I had the right to either temporarily relocate at the landlord's expense while an air filtration system was installed, or permanently relocate without repercussion.

I chose, of course, to permanently relocate. That relocation turned out to be the gateway to bringing into my life everything I've ever wanted: the first safe, supportive relationship of my life; a home on the water in the country; the opportunity to leave the medical transcription world and start a business helping women heal from trauma; excellent health, with an end to my lifelong anxiety and chronic pain; and the chance to help my children heal and thrive.

On New Year's Eve in 2013, I thought I was making a simple choice to ease my grief and anger, a choice to give myself a little breathing room for the first time in almost a year. In reality, that in-the-moment choice was the Divine guiding me to the intuitive knowing that formed the key to changing my life: everything is energy, and purposefully choosing the energy you bring in through your thoughts, emotions, and actions has the power to create miracles.

REFLECTIONS

Katt experienced an avalanche of loss in a short period of time. Have you experienced too many changes at once? How did you navigate the shifting sands of your life?

_____

_____

_____

_____

In choosing to make her dog Maverick's last days peaceful and beautiful, Katt chose those things for herself as well. Has a choice you made for someone else ever turned out to be a choice for you?

_____

_____

_____

_____

Katt chose Samhain and the Wheel of the Year to mark the point of new beginnings for her. What dates and rituals do you connect to? How do you use them in your spiritual practices to create powerful shifts?

_____

_____

_____

_____

LIGHT IN THE DREAM OF DESPAIR

Monica Dubay

*A*nother night of panic, lying awake dreading the next day, and thinking, *All I want to do is die.*

How did I get here? I am thirty years old, it is 1989, and I am married and working in New York City as a technical writer for a major insurance company. My dream of being a musician has fizzled, and now I sit alone all day in my cubicle, watching the clock.

On top of this, after a second miscarriage, I collapsed on the sidewalk with bags of groceries, doubled over in pain. I am one of nine children, and I imagined myself with at least two kids of my own. But now I go to work, come home, watch the news, make dinner and go to bed. I have trouble sleeping, and I can't shake the fear that my life seems to be unraveling.

My husband tries to help, but can't relate to me, so I see a doctor who diagnoses me with depression. I try the drugs and my feelings are masked by a dull cloud around my head, so I stop taking them.

Why am I so afraid? Why can't I sleep at night? I ask my therapist and she says, "Oh yes. A day without fear. Wouldn't that be nice?" No one seems to have the answer. She offers hypnosis and I accept. I begin to feel some relief, a few nights respite from sleeplessness. But the anxiety returns after a few days, and I feel hopeless again.

Maybe I will just get a disease and die, I think.

Someone at work shows me a book called *A Course in Miracles* and my first thought is that it looks like the Bible. I left Catholicism behind when I was in college, so I'm not interested. Instead, I search the self-help section in a nearby bookstore, and find a paperback called *You Can Heal Your Life* by Louise Hay.

"Your mind is a tool you can choose to use any way you wish," it states. "We create every so-called illness in our body. The body, like everything else in life, is a mirror of our inner thoughts and beliefs."

A bell goes off in my head: I have a disease, and it's up to me to change my thoughts. She states that *A Course in Miracles* tells us "all disease comes from a state of unforgiveness."

I listen to her meditation tapes each day and night. "Thank your bed, be grateful for your refrigerator, keep an open mind … You don't know what all the experiences today will be." I recall her soothing voice even now, almost three decades later.

I begin sleeping through the night.

I learn that my perception is caused by my thoughts and that I have to learn to change my beliefs if I want to recover. I admit I am deeply upset that my life didn't work out the way I wanted it to. I despair that I will never be a mother, and I don't know who to blame. Myself? For what? And what does forgiveness even mean? I need support.

I notice a class at the NY Open Center on *A Course in Miracles*. I feel a moment of terror, but know I need help, so I decide to sign up. During the first class, the teacher states that this book is radical and changes how you think. I buy it, take it home, and read the first of the 365 daily lessons in the Workbook.

The preamble states: "The opposite of love is fear, but what is all-encompassing can have no opposite." Love is the answer, and it is within you. Seek there and you will find it. It begins to make sense that we are created in love: it's what we are, and we simply need to align with this power within us for fear to disappear. Love and fear cannot coexist.

It sounds great, I think. *But will it help me?*

The lessons state that I have the power of decision: it's a universal Law of Mind that thoughts create experience. I have to take full responsibility for my thoughts, and then I will become free. This sounds too good to be true.

But I'm disciplined. I know that practicing something over time will produce results, so I apply the lessons to my daily life and discover there is another way to live, focusing on the release of fear instead of wallowing in it.

I begin to feel better and I want everyone to know! So I send the book to my mother and sister who love the Catholic Church; they both think I'm nuts. I continue doing the Workbook lessons every day and night for a few months, and become freer and happier than ever before in my life.

Then, suddenly, an unmistakable, commanding inner voice says to me loud and clear: "Go work for Marianne Williamson." I am astonished. *Who said that?* I don't know her personally at all—I am just doing some volunteer work for her organization, The Manhattan Center for Living. I visit people with AIDS in the hospital and I attend her lectures at Town Hall.

The voice says to write her and tell her exactly what is happening. So I do.

I sit down, shaking, scared out of my mind at how insane I must sound. I find out they have an opening at the Center for a volunteer coordinator. I write what the voice told me and send it to Marianne along with my resume. I don't know what will happen, but I have to do it anyway.

The next weekend, she is doing an intensive retreat and I sign up to volunteer. I run into her in the restroom and tell her that I had written the letter, and how weird I feel. She says, "Great. Get used to it, that's how this works."

The next thing I know, I've been hired. I am floored. Is this voice for real?

* * *

I loved working at the Center because, at last, I was given a reason to live. I was able to train volunteers and work for an organization that was doing something important. I spent my days in a healing environment which supported my growth, and I got to be of service to this devastated community.

I was asked to create a volunteer program that would serve people who were in pain, dying, and losing their loved ones to a dreadful disease. Marianne's vision was to provide counseling, bodywork, and a whole foods lunch program as well as support groups for people facing life-threatening illness. I loved it. My days were spent with people who wanted to help serve this community, and they inspired me.

Within a year, I got pregnant and had to make a very difficult choice: to keep this job, or stay home with my new baby. The birth of my first son showed me that I could create my life.

I was thrilled to be a mother. I listened to my inner voice and heart and chose to stay home with my son to give him the nurturing he needed. I had another baby two years later.

Then, the inner voice gave me another direction. "Go teach *A Course in Miracles*," it said to me. I resisted; I was more than terrified of public speaking. But I couldn't argue with the voice, so I put up a flyer and began teaching a weekly group in Brooklyn. I taught the lessons and spoke about my experiences of healing, and found that sharing the truth was powerful and helped me understand what was happening to me.

Over time, this first class led me to a life of teaching and healing. I have traveled to Europe, South America, and Australia to extend the message that you are not your thoughts: you are a divine being of love and are simply here to awaken to who you really are and realize the possibility of total freedom from fear.

My deepest pain allowed me to hit bottom and become forever changed. You need courage to face your anxiety, to go deep within and dig yourself out of depression. My hope is that this story helps you choose to be free, and know that no matter how dark it seems, there is help all around you and light within.

On that miraculous day when *A Course in Miracles* came into my life, I received a real answer to my painful cry for help. The message of the Course is simple: Love is the answer, and it is what you are. Identify with love and find yourself.

REFLECTIONS

What would it be like to live without fear?

_____

_____

_____

_____

Monica found healing in two profound books, and the practices she learned there. Where do you look for healing and inspiration?

_____

_____

_____

_____

Monica found that teaching A Course in Miracles helped her to better understand her own journey. How can you teach from your truth to help others and yourself?

_____

_____

_____

_____

CHAPTER

five

THE COURAGE TO MOVE FORWARD

SPRING IS COMING

Lisa Marie Rosati

My plane touched down at 10:57 p.m. on March 3. I was grateful to be home after a full day of plane travel from San Antonio, Texas to Southwest Florida. My back was screaming from sleeping on a different mattress for four nights, and the thought of sleeping in my own bed brought a sweet smile of relief to my lips.

As soon as I heard the landing wheels hit the runway, I turned on my cellphone. One by one, the text messages I'd received during the flight began to roll in. There were some business related messages, a text from my mom, and a group text from my three kids checking in on me. Then, a few seconds later, a message from my husband, informing me that our neighbors would be picking me up because he had eaten sushi for dinner and was on the toilet with the runs.

My first thought was, *Eeew*! My second was, *How inconsiderate!* I mean, I was away for five days, and he's in no rush to see me? I didn't appreciate this shenanigan one little bit.

Over the last decade, my husband and I had definitely had our ups and downs. However, our relationship had taken a marked downward turn in the last six months—ever since he retired and we decided to move from New York to Florida. That wasn't an easy decision for me, especially since it involved making arrangements for my teenage boys to live with their biological father, but I decided to put my marriage first, and give this new chapter of our lives a try. After twenty-seven years of being a mama, I was moving to paradise to live it up as an empty-nester!

I was hoping that being together in Florida would improve our relationship, but the opposite happened. In New York, he'd spend twelve hours a day working at our self-defense school, while I devoted my time to my kids and my business. Now, though, we were holed up in our new house together twenty-four hours a day. We had never spent so much concentrated time together. He was reclusive by nature, and never wanted to go anywhere or socialize with anyone. I was away from everything and everyone I knew, and going out alone to explore wasn't comfortable for me. I began to resent our new life, and feel trapped despite our beautiful surroundings.

The real kicker, though, was that, as the months went on, I realized I didn't actually enjoy spending time alone with my man. Not one little bit. As the rose-colored glasses finally came off, I started to lose trust in him, and even to dislike him as a person. Everything he said or did became annoying to me on a cellular level. I didn't want to be the one to break my commitment to our marriage, but I started begging him to "let me go" during our arguments. Every time we fought, the atmosphere grew colder and more distant.

Yes, we were in sunny paradise, but winter had set in—and this time, I didn't think spring was coming back around again.

So when my husband wasn't at the airport to pick me up after we'd spent the last five days apart, it was another nail in the proverbial coffin. Thank the gods my neighbors were waiting for me outside the airport. Even at 11:00 p.m., they were upbeat and chatty on the way home; I was not. I was planning my next move. Should I just say hello and go to bed, or should I tell him how I really felt and deal with the ensuing fireworks?

As the garage door opened slowly, I decided I was too tired to fight, and that Option Number One—bed—was the better choice. I steeled myself and plotted my path from kitchen to bathroom to bedroom.

The moment I stepped inside, the alarm triggered, and I knew something was wrong.

The dogs were in their crates. When I turned on the lights in the kitchen and great room, the house seemed dead. Then, I saw the note on the dining room table, and the set of keys on top.

The next few moments were a blur as my mind struggled to put the pieces together. There was only one conclusion I could come to: my husband of ten years had just left me while I was on a business trip.

My neighbor hugged me good night, which snapped me out of my trance. After she left through the garage, I went back to the table, and stood there staring at the note. After what felt like an hour, I finally picked it up.

The man with whom I'd spent the last decade of my life had actually typed me a Dear Jane letter, and printed it out. I didn't even warrant a handwritten note, apparently. Looking back now, I have to laugh; it was just so cliché. But at the time, it was devastating.

I called my mom and dad. They were in the car and on their way within ten minutes, and stayed with me all night as I cried out my deep feelings of betrayal and disbelief.

The next few days were excruciatingly painful for me. Mentally, I'd known this was a possibility, but that didn't stop me from feeling like my entire life had just imploded. I was beyond scared and totally triggered. *Who is going to love me and take care of me?* I wondered. I couldn't stop the toxic loop of my fearful thoughts. My beautiful new home became an empty, dark cavern where I felt freezing cold and very, very alone. All I could think was, *I hate it here!*

I stopped eating, managing only to get fluids and some soup down from time to time during the day. At night, I would lay in my bed staring at the ceiling, shivering and sobbing. To say I was experiencing a "dark night of the soul" would be a massive understatement. I felt like I was traversing the underworld naked and barefoot.

After a while, I noticed that I was allowing a terrible thought to take root: *All men are untrustworthy*. At first, I liked thinking that thought, because it allowed me to focus my anger and betrayal on all men, not just the one. I found myself repeating it like a mantra.

But then, over the next few weeks, something miraculous began to happen. Honorable, trustworthy men began showing up, quite literally, at my front door. I noticed that my dad would hug me for just a little bit longer than usual, and that he used kinder words. When my girlfriends stopped over to check in on me, their husbands would hug me, look me in the eyes, and assure me that a "real man" would never choose the cowardly exit that my husband did. The workmen in charge of my pool installation made sure that everything was taken care of just so. The landscape foreman told me that he wanted his design of my garden beds to make me feel special and loved.

And, most comforting of all, my two sons spent hours on the phone with me, assuring me that everything would be all right—and that when the time was right, and I met a man who was worthy of my love, they would be happy for me. I didn't believe that I would find someone, but I did allow myself to buy into the idea. I loved that my kids wanted me to be happy again.

Around this time, I started to wonder, what *would* make me happy? I thought about how I'd made so many excuses in my relationship, and how I'd minimized core components of a real partnership—like trust, laughter, kindness, and intimacy. Looking back, it was a big mistake on my part not to prioritize those things. It's a mistake I will never make again.

It took about two weeks of deep inner suffering before I felt ready to get out into the world again, and recreate my life. I was scared to death, but I was sick of hiding out with my fearful thoughts. It was time to move again.

One of my goals for my time in Florida was to invest in some income properties, so I put myself into real estate school. I also put up a profile on an online dating website. I figured I had a choice: I could put myself back in the game of love with an open heart, trusting what was meant to be, or stay holed up alone and let this painful experience ruin me for relationships forever.

I put up a profile on Match.com, and my inbox started filling up within the hour. Within a couple of days, I'd had pleasant Internet chats with quite a few men, as well as invites to go out on dates. It took me a bit by surprise, but it was great to get out of my shell and meet some new people.

I never imagined myself starting over at nearly fifty years of age, but that's life for you: it's unpredictable, it's messy, and it's always surprising. This new chapter had a rocky start, for sure, but I feel more alive, loved, and cared for than I ever have in my life. I've had to be brave, and step way out of my comfort zone. When I did so, I felt like I started finding bits and pieces of myself that I had forgotten about for years.

Someday soon, I'm sure I'll have a steamy chapter to share about how I found real love again—but for now, I'm enjoying the new adventure. Spring is coming, and I'm ready to bloom like never before.

REFLECTIONS

Has the end of a relationship ever taken you by surprise? What was your reaction? What beliefs were formed as a result of this experience?

_____

_____

_____

_____

Lisa realized that she had been tolerating a lack of core components in her relationships. Are you de-prioritizing important energies in your own life or relationships? How can you bring these things forward?

_____

_____

_____

_____

When you picture yourself "blooming," what do you envision?

_____

_____

_____

_____

BIRTH OF THE HIGHLY SENSITIVE BADASS

Cortney Chaite

I sat there, staring at my computer screen. My hand hovered over the "Send" button as my heart raced and my mind screamed, "You don't have to do this. It's okay just to live a simple, easy life. You don't have to put yourself out there."

I reread the e-mail I was about to send.

> *Hi, Stuart.*
>
> *I'm so excited to work with you on designing my new logo and website! I'm sending the deposit today, and I can't wait to bring The Highly Sensitive Badass to the world!*

Gulp. Quick breaths.

"Oh my God. What the hell am I doing?"

Send.

Every part of my mind and body screamed in fear, but I knew I had to do it. This was the next step in my evolution. It was the next step for my coaching practice. It was the next step towards my life's purpose. It was time for me to "come out of the closet" and serve sensitive female entrepreneurs as my whole, sensitive, empathic, and strong self. It was time for me to be brave and courageous, stepping through my fear and into a greater version of myself.

Never in my life had I taken such a big risk. Oh, there had been other risks: marriage and kids come to mind immediately, but this was a risk of a different magnitude. This was opening myself up, putting myself out there, and telling my truth in the most vulnerable way ... publicly.

I felt as though I had opened the door to be judged, criticized, ridiculed, and possibly laughed at by those who wouldn't understand what it was to be a sensitive and empathic person.

But there was more. As a highly sensitive person, I was terrified of taking on too much. I spent the past few years learning how to thrive as a sensitive person, mastering self-care and self-love, and I was feeling great.

When I was thirty-five and a stay-at-home mom with two young kids, my health started failing. I had neurological symptoms, intense anxiety, digestive issues, dizziness, and extreme fatigue. This was the first turning point guiding me toward my future: I devoted myself to overhauling my diet as I worked with a chiropractor. With my health, energy, and vitality restored, I realized the power of food and became a health coach.

However, I still struggled with the balance between taking care of myself and running a coaching practice. As a highly sensitive person, I never realized how much self-care I truly needed to thrive until I learned how to give it to myself. I had improved my diet, but I was still missing so many self-care tools and practices. Once I began implementing them, I found peace and strength through soul nourishment, the practice of pleasure, self-love, and acceptance. In addition to my new, healthy diet, these became my self-care practices. I felt the best I could remember feeling in my forty-two years on this planet.

So, I found myself terrified by the idea of rocking the boat.

What if I couldn't handle the workload? What if I felt overwhelmed? What if I couldn't show up and deliver? What if

I failed? What if I experienced depression or anxiety?

Could I do this?

A few years earlier, when I started my career in coaching, I was focused solely on health coaching as I worked with women to improve their health through changes in how and what they were eating. However, I quickly felt overwhelmed by coaching. I had a yearning to help people transform, but I didn't know how to be myself and have a career. I didn't know how to show up for people on the days when I was feeling overwhelmed by all the responsibilities in my life. A difficult morning getting a child to school could impact how I felt for the entire day. I was also so affected by the challenges my clients faced. My empathy had a tendency to take over, preventing me from staying grounded in my energy. I still showed up, but it was at the expense of myself. I often felt drained and exhausted instead of purposeful and motivated. I lacked the boundaries I needed to coach effectively while also taking care of myself and my family. The truth is that for a long time, I felt I couldn't be a coach because of my sensitivity and empathy. I felt like I didn't "have it all together."

So I stopped coaching. I thought, *I guess this isn't for me. I'm just not suited for this.* Along with those thoughts came deep shame, self-judgment, and feelings of failure that I couldn't do the one thing I passionately wanted to do.

Or so I thought.

I felt as though my sensitivity prevented me from having the career of my dreams. My flawed thinking was that I needed to cure myself of my sensitive nature so that I could be the best coach I could be. I viewed my sensitivity as a curse and a burden. I thought, *I'm too empathic to coach. I'm too feeling. I can't handle it.*

I hid this side of myself, and I kept it in the dark. I kept myself small and stuck. I didn't realize that if I bravely claimed it, I would find strength and empowerment.

What I didn't realize back then is that my sensitivity is my superpower. My empathy, my compassion, my experience, my vulnerability, and my authenticity have the power to make me the very best coach to someone else who is sensitive and struggling, but who has an inner fire to make a difference. By being my whole self, I have the power to help other sensitive entrepreneurs heal and feel whole.

If I denied this part of me, it showed others that they also had to deny this part of themselves. So instead of running from it, I embraced it. I also embraced new tools and self-care practices that allowed me to show up powerfully. I was ready to go full-throttle.

But then, there I was, ready to jump back in with my heart on my sleeve, and I was *terrified*. I was afraid of melting down, taking on too much, and letting down my clients. I was afraid of being judged, laughed at, getting funny looks from friends and family.

The ultimate fear came down to this question: Could I still honor myself and truly be the authentic "me" and sustain a business at the same time?

It turns out, the answer is yes.

The answer is yes because living my truth and being my most authentic self means that I can be highly sensitive, deeply feeling, brilliant, loving, silly, and compassionate, and still occasionally experience depression and self-doubt. More, I can do this while serving my divinely contracted clients—sensitive entrepreneurs who are here to make a big impact. By speaking my truth, I can bring all of myself to my work because I don't have to hide. I can be my whole, perfectly imperfect self.

By speaking my truth, I am speaking to those who speak the same soul language that I do, and I can connect to those I am meant to serve in a way I never could when I was hiding behind the façade of, "Everything is great all the time! I've got everything under control. Don't worry about me! Things are perfect over here!"

Living courageously doesn't mean that you'll never experience fear. It means bringing all parts of yourself to the table despite your fear. It means embracing imperfection as perfection. It means being vulnerable and strong. It means finding the beauty in your shadow so you can shine your light.

REFLECTIONS

If you were to honor yourself and your self-care needs as the ultimate priority, how would your life transform? What would become possible for you that isn't possible now?

_____

_____

_____

_____

Cortney writes about learning to embrace parts of herself that she hid and shunned for years. What parts of yourself are you denying or running away from? What would happen if you embraced these parts of yourself?

_____

_____

_____

_____

If you had no fear and could speak your truth with no repercussions, what would your message to the world be?

_____

_____

_____

_____

A MOTHER'S JOURNEY

Katrina Burton

When I reflect on courageous moments in my life, there are many experiences that come to mind. There are times from my younger years, like the first time I swam across the deep end of the pool, or dove off the high diving board. There are more from my adulthood, like the agonizing process of awaiting medical results, or standing up for myself in hostile work situations.

Yet, when I think about my most courageous moments, there is a difference. There are certain pivotal moments in my life when everything changed. If I were writing my life story, there would be distinct lines in the sand that differentiate life before and after these events. These events shape who I am, provide strength for me to draw upon, and equip me to connect with others during their most intimate and authentic expressions of joy, pain, and existence.

By far, the most courageous and defining moment of my life was the time I lost my mother and became a mother, all at the same time.

My mom and I were super close. She was my best friend and the wind beneath my wings. She had a very nurturing presence, and I always felt safe and secure around her. I remember watching the Mary Tyler Moore show with her in the mornings when I was a little girl. These were my favorite memories ever. Life was so happy, so full, so safe, so joyful!

There was so much about her that I took for granted when she was here. I look back now on the sacrifices she made so that my brother and I could have a good quality of life. She was the mom who drove us and our friends across the inner city to dance practices and football games. Everyone loved her, and she constantly did kind things as an expression of her love and compassion for others. It meant the world to have a person in my life who I knew had my back no matter what. She was my rock, and I knew that everything would always be okay as long as she was around.

This may explain why it came as such a shock to learn that she was sick. It came out of nowhere. I was in my mid-twenties and out shopping for patio furniture one evening when my cell phone rang. It was my newlywed husband, David, calling to tell me that my mom was in the hospital. Apparently, she had not been feeling well and had gone to the emergency room to be evaluated. After a few long days of medical testing, we received the devastating news that she had lung cancer. She had been a cigarette smoker since her teenage years. We had always begged her to stop smoking, yet we never expected this news. She still seemed healthy, vibrant, and full of life.

It was so painful to watch her endure the torture of chemotherapy and radiation. More than the hair she lost, or the many pounds she shed, it was so unsettling to watch her lose her essence. That sense of nurture and calm which she always exuded grew dim. She was busy, after all, battling for her life. Looking back, I am certain that at some point she realized she was not going to beat her illness. Yet I think she knew the pain of this reality would be too much for us to bear, so she kept it inside. Throughout the ordeal, I maintained faith that she would be healed.

A little over a year after my mom's diagnosis, my husband and I made the courageous decision to try to start a family. We had been married for two years and felt ready. Moreover, my mom had always wanted a grandchild, and we felt that the excitement of a new little bundle of love in the family would bring her joy. Selfishly, we hoped she might find new determination and inspiration to beat cancer! I can still remember the tears that flowed down my mom's cheeks the moment she learned she was going to be a grandmother. She was so happy, and it did renew her motivation to beat her illness. But there are our plans, and then there are God's plans.

I remember when I received the news that I needed to go the hospital. My friends had just hosted the most beautiful baby shower for David and me. I called to share the wonderful news with my mom and tell her about the lovely gifts we received. But my dad answered, and he told me she was not doing well. I could tell in his voice that things were not good. She had been recently hospitalized as she was having trouble walking. I had briefly spoken with her earlier that day, but within a flash she had suddenly taken a turn for the worse.

David and I made the torturous drive to the hospital as quickly as we could. My brother, aunt, and uncle all arrived at the hospital at the same time we did. When we entered my mom's hospital room, we knew immediately that things were not good. She was no longer conscious, and oxygen machines kept her breathing. The sound of her heavy and labored breathing on those machines was heart-wrenching.

Nine months pregnant at the time, I took her hand and lay by her bedside. I hummed the only song which could bring me peace in that moment.

Oh the blood of Jesus. Oh, the blood of Jesus.
Oh, the blood of Jesus. It washes white as snow.
There is power, power, wonder-working power,
in the blood of the lamb.

As I sang to her for what felt like hours, I could feel the sense of peace come over her as her breathing settled and calmed. It brought me such fulfillment to be a source of peace and calm for her in that moment in the same way she had always been for me. She slipped away quietly and peacefully, leaving each of our lives fractured in a way that would never be the same.

My mom never lived to see the birth of her first grandchild. Kiarra was born three weeks after my mother's passing. Losing my mother and becoming a mother at the same time was the most difficult thing I have ever done. I didn't know anything about taking care of a baby or being a mother. In the days, weeks, and months to come, I would have to dig to the deepest depths to find the strength to care for this baby who demanded so much, all while I was experiencing the most painful grief of my life. I learned how to be a mother while mourning the loss of the exact person who could have helped me the most. I experienced the deepest emotional pain of losing my mom, and the most sacred joy of becoming a mother, all at once.

I struggled with my faith for a while trying to understand why everything happened as it did. Why didn't my mom live to see the birth of her granddaughter? Couldn't she have at least had one chance to hold Kiarra in her arms? A good friend helped me to reframe this. My mom did, in fact, see Kiarra, before we ever did. Before Kiarra came to this side of creation, she and my mom connected in the spiritual realm. My mother saw her and held her there, and a special part of my mother lives on in our hearts through the blessing we received in Kiarra.

No matter the difficulty we face in life, God always provides a way for us to endure. Kiarra was a gift that helped all of us to get through the most difficult of times. I am eternally grateful for the blessing of the joy of becoming a mother just when I needed the strength to bear the grief of losing mine. It was just the gift I needed to cross that line in the sand.

Seventeen years later, I look in Kiarra's face, as well as the face of her younger sister Karyssa, who came four years later, and I am thankful for my beautiful daughters, as well as the beautiful angel watching us all from above.

REFLECTIONS

What are your "line in the sand" experiences—the times when you stepped forward in courage and changed your life forever?

_____

_____

_____

_____

What provides you with comfort and wisdom during difficult times?

_____

_____

_____

_____

Consider one of your life's biggest challenges. Was there a gift that came alongside that challenge? How might that challenge and that gift help give you strength in the future?

_____

_____

_____

_____

THE ROAD TO BALANCE

Jennifer Flynn

*M*ore than any part of the day, I dreaded the mornings. The sun coming up was simply a sign of yet another day with more overwhelm, more dissatisfaction and utter lack of fulfillment … just more blah blah blah. I was in survival mode, just getting by.

Each day, in the moments between dropping the kids at school and arriving at work; in the office bathroom; when everyone else was at lunch and I was still working; on the way home; in the shower; and in those moments before utter exhaustion finally took hold for the night, I cried. I have never been a "crier," yet the supply of tears seemed never to end!

Every day started to look like the next. Trying to pretend everything was okay, even though we all knew it wasn't because I was ripping everyone's face off before we even got to the car. Digging my nails into my palms while my hands wrapped around the steering wheel to the point of pain, forcing me to think about something else so I could prevent the tears from falling before I could get the kids out of the car at school. I hated that nothing was changing. I felt trapped in a job I was exceedingly good at but no longer loved the income and the responsibilities.

"Breathe, just breathe," I would tell myself, counting down: only five more miles, six more blocks, then three, then two, then everyone out of the car. I would park at the end of the block to get the sobs out before I walked into work, hoping no one would see me. I needed the air hitting my face for the short walk to carry away as much of what I was feeling as possible and cool down my red, hot face. One block never seemed to be enough to brush away the utter despair and nausea that I felt entering the building every day. Another day of not being enough, of not being able to get my arms around a job that had gotten too big for me. I worried that speaking up for myself sounded like whining because I still managed to get everything done. To others, it seemed like I was handling everything just fine. Yet, I didn't feel heard or that I was being taken seriously.

Everyone always complimented me on how well-put-together I was and how I could get anything done and made everything look easy. As the primary breadwinner for my family, that just added to the pressure and amplified my lifelong perfectionism. I felt like the weight of all the stress was going to suffocate me. I was too good at too many things, and if I'm being honest, I had become a control enthusiast as a result. I spun too many plates. Trying to be perfect at everything and always be "enough" were strangling me. Every time I turned around, a plate was falling; I swept it up and set another one spinning before anyone noticed. The problem: I noticed. Which just added to my stress and constant overwhelm.

I hit critical mass with my pain and despair. My health, relationships, and happiness were suffering. I was angry. All. The. Time. The slightest thing could tip me into a maniacal rage. I had run out of tears, and I started to question my sanity. I could not find joy in anything anymore.

After a particularly tough week at work, I sat one Saturday afternoon in the middle of my living room floor wondering if I needed to go on antidepressants. I knew my level of stress was not normal and was no longer sustainable, yet I felt powerless against it. I did not want to turn to medication. I had done this for years before after my first daughter was born. I did not like the medicine's side effects, but what my children were witnessing was no longer acceptable. I did not want this to be their example of "normal." I also worried that if I went on medication, my husband would know just how bad it had gotten ... as if he didn't already.

I asked for an answer, a way out of the misery I was feeling. My soul was screaming for something bigger. My health was saying, "Don't wait too long."

When I listened, the answer that came sounded unbelievable to me. Who did I think I was?

The voice inside told me that I had always been a lighthouse for others. It was time to stop saying no when people asked me to work with them, and start saying yes to being more "me" than I had ever given myself permission to be.

I often heard, "I need you to coach me. Can I work with you?" I felt humbled by these requests, but insecure and like I wasn't enough. Who was I to tell other people how to live? I have often been in a position of people looking to me for a clearer path. It felt like the "calling" everyone talks about, but you can't support a family with a calling, so I spent most of my years minimizing the gifts everyone else saw.

I decided to distract myself from the negative internal self-talk by reading my e-mail. A time-sensitive offer for early-bird pricing on tuition to a coaching certification program I had been dancing around was waiting in my inbox for me. Was this a sign? Where would I find the money? Every penny was already accounted for. How could I consider making such a change when I was the primary breadwinner for my family? It felt selfish and too unpredictable. "Do not give up that stability," I would tell myself.

"Stability" seemed a bit relative at the moment, given I could see the future if unchanged playing out like a movie. If something did not change *now*, I would *not* be stable. I was going to lose it.

I called my husband at work and told him what I wanted to

do. I suggested that I use the truck for collateral and take out a loan to pay for the tuition. He was in total agreement. He just wanted to see me happy.

I balanced many spinning plates for the duration of my program. I stayed up until the wee hours every morning doing my homework and taking in everything I could. I started to put the word out quietly and the feedback I received was beyond my wildest imaginings. This actually made sense to other people! I felt so validated. I was worried that people would think I was crazy. Don't get me wrong, some did. The haters always sit in the front row, and yet, the overwhelming whole congratulated me and said things like, "That is who you have always been." "What a perfect fit!" and "How can I help?"

I still had to figure out how to transition out of my steady job without any loss in income. That feeling that I must be insane started to creep back in. I tried to remain still and listen for my true north. It said the same thing every time: "Go. Focus on the what. The how is on its way." Or, "Just shut up and trust me."

I have always been a decisive person when it comes to big things. I have a strong intuition and the good fortune of seldom being wrong about major decisions. I knew deep down better than to doubt myself. I just had to be clear in what I was asking for and how I wanted it to feel when it arrived.

I worked feverishly on packages and pricing, and second-guessed myself a thousand times. A thousand and one times, I silenced the gremlins of Guilt and Judgment who were trying to ride shotgun on this journey. My soul zone was finding its voice—and before I knew it, it was the loudest voice of all.

I managed to attract an opportunity to do some contract work in the coaching industry. That opportunity led me to others and within these were the people and skills I needed to grow my business. I coupled these experiences with what I already knew about running someone else's successful business and built my own from the ground up.

As I served private clients and those of companies I contracted with, I got deeper clarity that my biggest gift was in helping others end the war between work and play. Clients realized not only that could they have their cake and eat it too, but how they could do it with joy along the journey. I curated the keys to creating a life by design and being both personally and professionally fulfilled. In this space, The Balance Maven® was born followed by Balance YOUniversity™ where I teach busyaholic entrepreneurs and small business owners how to reach peak potential in their business and have plenty of time for leisure. They move from chaos and overwhelm to profitable, joyful work, with time to enjoy their leisure time guilt-free in all the ways that speak to their soul's calling. I understand this journey on a core level. It brings deep satisfaction to do this work with others, so they avoid the pitfalls and get there faster and more easily than I did.

I have built a successful business that supports my family in bigger ways than I ever imagined. The first full year on my own after leaving my job I doubled my income. I provide for my family better now than I did building someone else's dream. I can attend all of my children's important functions and extracurricular events, and allow two of my three daughters the opportunity to homeschool because I am in charge of my time and how I spend it. *I* decide how big I play this game we call life, and I help others do the same.

It has been said that if it doesn't scare you a little it probably isn't worth doing. It takes great courage to listen deeply to that voice inside. Sometimes you can barely hear it because it is hoarse after screaming at you for so long while you weren't listening. However, when you take the leap of faith and put all your trust in yourself, you never lose. You will always be your best bet.

REFLECTIONS

Jennifer writes about "spinning too many plates." Where in your life are you taking on too much? How can you set some of those responsibilities aside?

_____

_____

_____

_____

Are your dreams big enough, or are you playing "small and safe?"

_____

_____

_____

_____

What signs, offers, or opportunities are showing up for you right now? How can you act on them in an inspired way, right now?

_____

_____

_____

_____

FINDING MYSELF LOST

Kris Groth

I noticed heart-shaped rocks everywhere I looked. Surely this meant I was on the right path, despite not having seen tell-tale blazes marking my way. I'd already spent fifty minutes on what should have been an easy forty-five-minute hike. Where was the picturesque and peaceful lake? I wanted to sink into meditation while I sat on its shore instead of praying that my sandals, fine for an easy leisurely hike, would hold together until I arrived safely.

I paused at the top of yet another hill. Should I go back the way I'd come, or just cut across through the woods and meet up with the right path to the lake? For some reason, I felt compelled to go cut across the mountain. (I know what you may be thinking, that this was a really stupid thing to do, but at that moment I felt confident and had no doubt whatsoever that this was the right decision.)

I left the path and pushed through the woods. Tall pine trees towered over me as I traversed up the side of the mountain. The steep incline had a deep layer of pine needles and fallen dead branches which made it difficult to get solid footing. I trudged on, making as much noise as possible so I wouldn't startle any animals. I would crest one big hill and think the lake must be just over the next peak. But when I got to the top of each hill, the lake seemed to have moved.

Soon I was in a dense thicket as high as my waist, making it challenging to move. My long jeans kept my legs from being

183

shredded by the sharp branches. I had one bottle of water, a granola bar, and some nuts. Not knowing how long it would take to reach civilization, I conserved my resources, taking only sips of water when needed.

I crested one peak and discovered a steep, rocky crag. I thought if I could get to the top of it, I might be able to see which way to go. A couple of hours had passed. The sun was high in the sky and blazing down upon me. Nervous desperation filled me. I approached the rock wall I'd have to climb, and my fear kicked into overdrive. There could be mountain lions sunning themselves on the top. I could cause a rockslide, or find a sheer drop-off. I could fall to my death. But if I stayed at the bottom, I might never find my way out. A battle raged within me. I paced back and forth at the bottom of the rock ledge, panic building in my chest, heart racing.

Finally, I stopped and said to myself, "Okay, you can let your fear control you, stay lost, and possibly die, or you can take a chance trusting that you will be fine. What's it going to be?"

Memories flashed through my mind of all the fears that had been controlling me my whole life. Fear of failure, criticism, rejection, speaking, being seen, and being hurt. I was so limited by my fears, which made my life very small and constricted. Was this the way I wanted to live my life? No, I want to live a life that is big, bold, and without limitation. I felt my inner strength came in like a waterfall: calm, powerful, and strong.

"I can do this!" I told myself. "I will not be ruled by fear!"

I scaled the rock wall and made it to the top. No mountain lions. No lake either. I was lost! Nobody even knew where I was. I looked at my phone, thinking I should at least call someone to alert them to what was happening. No signal. On the edge of panic, I thought, *If you lose it and freak out you will not find your way back.* I took a deep breath, sat there calmly, and connected with myself. I called on my angels to be with me, to keep me safe, to guide me and help me find my way. I felt them gather around as a soft comforting presence, completely surrounding and enveloping me. It was like being wrapped in a warm blanket. Their gentle loving energy penetrated to my core melting my tension. I also felt supported by loving beings from the mountain there to protect me and show me the way. Suddenly I felt calm, safe, and confident that I would be okay. I gazed out over the vast forest and mountains. It saw a light shining in the distance. I knew that was the direction I needed to go.

I skittered down the steep mountainside but found again thick brush which I'd need to fight my way through. Feeling uncertain, I pulled out my phone and looked at its GPS. Despite having no cell service, I saw myself as a little blue dot in the middle of green mountains. I could also see the blue shape of the lake on the map. I felt more confident knowing I was going in the right direction, even if I had to go around some obstacles to reach the lake.

I trekked through the trees, rocks, brush, steep slopes, and hills for hours, before reaching a trickle of a rocky stream which I knew would lead me to the lake. I checked my magical GPS and confirmed the stream was indeed connected to the lake.

Taking no chances of getting lost again, I climbed into the stream and hiked its bed. About twenty minutes later, I went to check my GPS again. My phone was not in my pocket! This was my lifeline, my only hope, how could I lose it? My heart raced, and my chest tightened making it difficult to breathe.

As I looked back on where I had been, the forest seemed to swirl around me. I said a desperate little prayer as I retraced my steps through the stream, over rocks, and underbrush, trying to remember exactly where I had been. Lo and behold, my brightly-colored phone was beneath a bush I had crawled under! A huge sigh escaped me. Filled with gratitude and relief, I thanked my angels repeatedly for their help. I secured my phone, keeping my hand on it at all times, and proceeded back up the stream.

I wasn't sure what time the sun would set, but I felt like daylight must be running out. I finally found the lake, and the path I should have taken. I arrived at my car as the last bits of the sun were disappearing over the mountaintop. I had been lost for over six hours! I was so grateful to have made it, to be alive, and to be safe.

There were so many miracles that happened on the mountain. The heart-shaped rocks showed me I wasn't alone. The GPS that shouldn't have worked without a signal, yet still guided me to the lake. Finding my lost cell phone. My phone's charge lasting until the parking lot was in sight. My sandals hanging on by threads, yet still protecting my feet over all that rough terrain. Despite my mishap, I only ended up with a couple of blisters and no other injuries.

I know my angels were with me that day, keeping me safe, and protecting me. I also know that when I was so lost, I discovered strength in myself that I didn't know I had. Since that experience, when fear creeps up on me, I remind myself of my mountain adventure. If I can survive that, conquering all those dangers, I can do anything! I may have lost my way on the mountain, but I found my courageous heart. I will be forever grateful for that gift, and forever changed!

REFLECTIONS

When was the last time you were lost—physically or otherwise? How did you calm your fears?

_____

_____

_____

_____

When she felt panicked, Kris connected with her angels. How do you connect with your angels, guides, and teachers? How do they help you navigate?

_____

_____

_____

_____

When you've made a decision that didn't turn out as you intended, how have you corrected your trajectory to get back on the right path?

_____

_____

_____

_____

GO WEST, YOUNG WOMAN

Hedy MacDonald

I received the call while covering the reception desk at my midtown Manhattan job. I had been approved to lease a furnished studio apartment in sunny San Diego, so when did I want to move in?

Oh my God, this was it! How had I even gotten approved? Once I left New York City, I would have zero income until I found a new job in California. I hesitated for a moment. It sounded a little crazy. Was I sure this was what I wanted to do? Leave all my family and friends to move across the country to a place where I didn't know anyone, without having a job lined up?

Though the answer to that question seemed scary as hell, my dream was finally becoming a reality. I couldn't give up.

"In three-and-a-half weeks," I said.

When I walked back into my office, I had my resignation in hand. After leaving work, I had no time to waste thinking about how much my life was about to change. I ran to catch my train in order to make a shift at my second job, which began only 40 minutes later. After arriving at the bar, I changed into my cocktail waitress uniform before heading to the management office.

"I need to talk to you," I said.

"I need to talk to you, too," my manager said. "You go first."

I gave her my two-weeks notice.

Her jaw dropped. "You are leaving? But we were going to train you to be a bartender. Are you sure you won't reconsider?"

Free training to be a bartender was a tremendous offer and

had great income potential. By accepting her offer, I could save more money and be less rushed to find a job once I moved. Being a trained bartender would also give me more income potential once I arrived in California.

I considered it, but I couldn't bear the thought of another cold, dark winter or squeezing into another subway car with hundreds of strangers, like inmates being shipped to their prison for the day. I needed to be surrounded by colors, flowers, and warm weather as soon as possible. I knew San Diego was where I was meant to be and I didn't want to delay any further.

On that day, my world completely changed by me making bold decisions. But the hardest part was yet to come: telling my ten-year-old brother I would be moving. The last time I'd had to leave him occurred a few years earlier when I moved out of my parent's house into an apartment with my then fiancé. It was difficult to leave my brother, and we cried. But then, I was only a car drive away, and could spend every Saturday with him. Now there would be no option to see him every weekend.

I had become a big sister again at fifteen when my brother was born. He felt more like a son to me instead of a brother. It felt like I was abandoning him and I would have done anything to take him with me, but there was no way my parents would have let me take their youngest child away. Though I knew this move was the right thing to do, I wished with all my being that listening to my heart didn't have to entail breaking his.

The next three weeks I kept busy to keep my mind off of my sadness at leaving and worry about what was to come. I needed to purchase a car to drive across country with. I needed to decide which of my possessions meant enough to me to travel across the country and which would be left behind. Lastly, I needed to say goodbye to my beloved friends and family.

Though the weeks leading up to the move were nerve wracking, I knew without a doubt I was doing the right thing.

This calling of my heart and soul was so strong; I couldn't ignore it. It felt like the previous year had been a time for letting go of what no longer served me.

Just fourteen months earlier, I ended an unhealthy relationship with my first love, despite the fact I had made a commitment to love him in sickness and in health. Three months after the relationship ended, 9/11 happened, and that experience finalized my decision to leave the city. The months after that were spent working two jobs and partying with my friends to escape the fact that I was living back at home with my parents, and dreaming of the day I would finally leave New York and could start my life over from scratch, doing things my way.

Three weeks flew by in a blur and the time came for me to say goodbye. The image of my ten-year-old brother sitting on the couch, with a pained look in his eyes as I walked out the door for the last time, will forever be seared into my memory. To this day, I sob every single time I think of that moment. Choosing my heart, soul, and health over a loved one was absolutely heart-wrenching. Within the space of nearly a year, I had left two people I loved to listen to my heart.

Rebirthing myself and listening to the call of my soul was the hardest thing I have ever done. Family, friends, and acquaintances either thought I was crazy or admired me for my bravery. I didn't consider myself brave because I was living a truth that couldn't be ignored. It was time to take care of myself. It was time to rediscover who I was. It was time to live my life on my terms. It was time to start over anew without any of the old relationships, habits, and familiarity of the life I had been living by default up until this point.

The journey back to myself wasn't easy. When I first moved to San Diego, I set my alarm early every morning even though I had no place to go. I didn't want my depression to kick in, so I forced myself to get out of bed and get outside. I spent time in nature, doing things I loved like rollerblading and drawing.

Finding a job turned out to be a little harder than I had imagined. I borrowed one month's rent from a friend before I finally landed a job, which turned out to be a wonderful place where I met a lot of genuine people and made some great friends.

I'll never forget the outfit I wore the first day at work, something I would have never worn in New York: a bright yellow skirt with huge purple flowers splashed across it! Though wearing something so bold may seem like a small thing, my body image issues resulted in me often wearing black to blend in and help me look thinner. Choosing to wear this outfit was a huge statement for me. I told myself that it was time to wear and do what brought me joy regardless of what others thought.

Two years after moving to San Diego, I met my husband. We hit it off right away and were married within a year. We currently live with our two kids in the middle of a forest on the west coast. I have my own business coaching others and doing energy work, something I never in a million years would have thought I would be doing.

My youngest brother now lives on the west coast as well. He travels all the time and listens to the call of his heart and soul. I like to think that, perhaps, he learned this lesson from me. Maybe he didn't; either way, it was a lesson I had to learn. Taking that huge leap and act of faith to learn was the only way I could learn to listen to my heart and soul 100 percent.

Because I listened to the callings of my soul, I know that no dream is too small, and that I can accomplish anything. Following my heart may have been painful, but it was worth it to be true to myself. Most importantly, I know that though playing small feels comfortable, courageous acts are what took me home to myself.

REFLECTIONS

Have you ever felt you were living in the wrong place? What did that feel like? How did you respond to that knowledge?

Leaving loved ones is incredibly difficult. Have you ever had to tell someone you were moving (or moving on)? How did you prepare for that conversation?

If you could live in perfect authenticity, anywhere in the world, where would you be? What about that place would feel like home to you?

EDITOR'S NOTE

Bryna René Haynes, *Chief Editor*

*T*his past year, I found the courage to do something I have historically sucked at.

It wasn't easy, and I struggled with my choice for a long time. I stayed up nights mulling it over in my head, wondering if it was the wrong way to go, wondering if I was setting myself up for disappointment. Wondering if I should just suck it up and do what I've always done, instead of embracing this new, scary, unknown way.

What was this choice I made, you ask? What was so big and scary that it tore holes in my world?

I asked for help. In my *business*.

(Cue dramatic music.)

Don't laugh. I know it sounds crazy, but my work was the one place in my life that, up until this year, I retained the control-freakism and perfectionist narrative that used to rule my entire life. I mean, we're talking about my purpose, my passion, and my *life's work* here—not to mention my income.

Yes, I was locked into that insidious (and ridiculous) small-business-owner mindset that says, "No one can do what I do like I do it." More, I was struggling with decades-old trust issues. It felt like I had a case of what my toddler calls the "icky-yicky-gummy-stickies."

Nevertheless, I took the leap. I asked for help—and help arrived, in the form of my Heart of Writing team, brilliant collaborators, and talented friends. As I let go of some of my cherished responsibilities,

I discovered that while it may actually be true that no one can do what I do exactly like I do it, that's not a bad thing. All it means is that each of my collaborators and Team members work in their own inspired, totally amazing ways, and rock my world in the process. Seriously. I've been blown away.

"But what," you ask, "does all of this have to do with *Courageous Hearts* and the stories these brave authors have contributed?"

Everything!

You see, I've been Inspired Living Publishing's Chief Editor since 2010, but this was the first time I've asked for extensive help with one of our collaborative books. My second daughter was due to be born smack in the middle of our editing schedule, and there simply was no way I could juggle a newborn and give our authors the support they needed and deserved. How was I going to make this work?

Before I could go into panic mode, our beloved publisher, Linda Joy (who always manages to talk me off the ledge when I get stressed), called me to say that she had met a woman who would be a fabulous addition to our editing team. Talk about divine timing!

And so it was that ILP Associate Editor Deborah Kevin joined our team just in time to save my butt. She dove in with total confidence and abandon, and her attention to detail shines through in the quality of the stories she oversaw. She most certainly made *Courageous Hearts* an even more powerful book by her contribution, and I can't wait to work with her on future projects.

But that's not all. In addition to Deborah's near-miraculous appearance, I also received incredible support from my Heart of Writing Team member Rebecca van Laer, PhD, writer/editor *extraordinaire*, whose line edits helped take the stories of nineteen of our authors to the next level. She stepped in to fill her role with ease and grace, and her compassionate heart and massive skill set shone through in every interaction. Rebecca, I can't thank you enough. I'm so honored to call you my friend and collaborator.

As I navigated this project and my new *modus operandi*, I discovered the true gift of a courageous heart: the ability to transcend limitations, shed doubts like an old skin, and step into something bigger and better than I could have dreamed. It is, to quote my teenage self, "wicked friggin' awesome."

It's no accident that my personal revelation coincided with this particular project. All of Inspired Living Publishing's books have a way of seeping into the consciousness of their authors—and by extension, their editors. Their themes are always timely, their contributors always divinely inspired. The incredible authors who shared their stories here did so not only because they needed to write them, but because we needed to read them; it's a synchronicity that Linda Joy has created and continues to nurture.

At this moment, my six-week-old Little Star is stretched out on her nursing pillow across my lap, cooing at me as I type over her head. She loves "working" with me, as for her it usually involves eating, snuggling, and snoozing, her three favorite activities.

"It's a crazy, amazing life you've chosen," I tell her. "But you'll never have to go it alone. We can be brave together."

She smiles, smacks her rosebud lips, and falls back to sleep.

Trust. It's a beautiful thing.

Bryna René Haynes
Chief Editor, Inspired Living Publishing

ABOUT OUR AUTHORS

TARAH ABRAM is a designer, photographer, advocate for wellness and lifestyle coach. She is passionate about helping busy and overwhelmed moms who want to transition themselves and their families to a more holistic and juicier way of living and design a beautiful, healthy lifestyle. She focus on the areas of mind, body, and the environment that surrounds you. Learn more at www.JuicyLivingByDesign.com and claim your free gift!

FELICIA BAUCOM is passionate about helping women connect with the truth of who they are and make bold decisions so they can create the fulfilling and authentic lives they long for. She left her twenty-year career in corporate America to empower women who want to achieve their visions and look forward to their lives. She encourages women to lessen distractions, listen to their highest calling, and be the hero of their own lives. Learn more at www.MarchToYourOwnDrum.com and download your free gift "5 Ways to Create A Life You LOVE."

KATRINA BURTON is the founder of ReAuthor Your Story Coaching, LLC. She is a Certified High Performance Coach™ specializing in transformational coaching to help clients redesign their lives in alignment with their highest selves. Katrina lives in Ellicott City, Maryland with her husband, David, and their two daughters. Connect with Katrina at www.KatrinaBurton.com and download your free e-book, "The Five Keys to ReAuthoring Your Story" today!

SHEILA CALLAHAM is an international best-selling author and motivational coach. She founded the Activate Your Braveheart program to help women identify hidden passions and find the courage to make them real. Sheila's mission is to empower women through writing, speaking, and coaching. Visit her website at www.ActivateYourBraveheart.com and claim your free "Activate Your Braveheart™ Transformation Kit" today.

CORTNEY CHAITE is an international Mindset, Life and Health Coach for Heart-Centered Women. She is also a writer, speaker, mentor and advocate for Highly Sensitive, Empathic, Intuitive and Spiritual People. Her passion is helping women achieve more success in their business and more happiness in their lives through divine self-care, mindset coaching and manifesting so they can live their highest purpose and reach their full potential. www.TheHighlySensitiveBadass.com.

FELICIA D'HAITI is a Feng Shui and Soul Coach who guides clients in shifting their perspectives and environments to move beyond perfectionism, fear and self-imposed limitations. Felicia is an educator, Feng Shui, Space Clearing, and Soul Coaching® Teacher. She is a contributing author in *Midlife Transformation* and other best-selling books. She lives in Maryland with her husband and four children. Learn more at www.FeliciaDHaiti.com and download her "Get Clear on Your Space Feng Shui Starter Kit."

Through her own experiences of addiction, depression, and loss, MAL DUANE has transformed her life and recreated herself as an awakened, authentic woman. Now, she helps women heal their broken hearts and reclaim their lives. A best-selling author, inspirational speaker, and coach, she has been featured on Fox News, CBS Radio, and over 200 Internet radio shows, and is a contributor to MariaShriver.com, Healthy Living, and Aspire Magazine. You can reach Mal on www.MalDuaneCoach.com.

MONICA DUBAY is a spiritual life coach, energy healer and founder of Heal Your Mind, Heal Your Life, a powerful Transformation Program that helps people crush fear, shamelessly love themselves, and change the world by changing their beliefs. She has been a teacher of *A Course in Miracles* since 1990, after being completely and miraculously healed of anxiety and depression. A masterful healer, Monica helps people discover who they really are and embrace their true life's purpose by combining spiritual wisdom and business coaching. Visit www.HealYourMindHealYourLife.com to claim your "Ten Steps to Create Your Life's Desire" Workbook and "Meditation to Release 11 Self-Sabotaging Beliefs."

ERIN ESSER is a soul-centered coach, a Reiki Master/teacher and the creator of the highly transformative program, Awaken Your Purpose, where she helps women get in touch with their unique brilliance in the themselves, stop sabotaging, and learn self-compassion so they can be of the highest service to the world! Erin offers online sessions privately or in small groups, leads full and new moon circles each month within her community, and hosts the podcast, "Your Sacred Witness." Erin lives in North Carolina with her three kiddos and two dogs. You can find her at www.ErinEsser.com

JENNIFER FLYNN, a business and lifestyle strategist, specializes in helping overwhelmed entrepreneurs and small business owners end the war between work and play. She is the owner of The Balance Maven® and creator of the signature program Balance YOUniversity™. Her clients enjoy effective systems that streamline for efficiency and end overwhelm one step at a time. In maximizing productivity, more free time couples with profitable results leading to increased personal fulfillment and a healthier business. Learn more at www.TheBalanceMaven.com and claim your complimentary "get acquainted" call.

KRIS GROTH is a spiritual mentor, craniosacral energy healer, intuitive artist, and writer. She is passionate about helping people connect more deeply to their own essence and spirit, assisting them to receive guidance and clarity about their soul's path and purpose, promoting healing and restoring balance to the body, mind, heart, and soul. Kris offers healing/mentoring sessions in-person and by phone, and guided sound healing meditations using crystal singing bowls. Learn more at www.KrisGroth.com and claim your free Sacred Sound Healing Meditation & Affirmation Gift Set!

JAMI HEARN is passionate about supporting women in clearing the blocks and restrictions holding them back from living their divinity and aligning with and attracting their divine abundance. As a lawyer who felt unfulfilled on a soul level, Jami's own journey led her to become a Certified Soul Realignment Practitioner and Akashic Records Reader, and today her thriving practice supports other women in living their soul's purpose. Learn more at www.LiveYourDivinity.com and download your "Meet Your Abundance Guide" meditation.

Family health expert AMANDA HINMAN is passionate about allowing parents everywhere to enjoy their most important job: raising a vibrant child! A sought-after speaker and author of *Vibrant Child: 7 Steps to Increase Your Child's Health & Happiness,* she created a proven process to transform hundreds of moms from frustrated and overwhelmed to confident and empowered. Her strategies empower you to solve the stress. Say good-bye to arguments and meltdowns and hello to *clarity* and *more time for yourself* when you claim your free "Vibrant Child Starter Kit" today at www.Hinmans.com.

Transformational CINDY HIVELY is a renowned Healing Catalyst for Spiritual Women. She's the Priestess and Goddess Creatrix for her brand In Her Fullness, an Intuitive Healing Coach, columnist for *Aspire Magazine* and best-selling author. She helps women remove blockages, and optimize each key area of life by using her signature process, Nature and Creation Alchemy. She shows women how to create healing using everyday modalities with magical ritual. It's Cindy's life passion and soul work to help women experience a luscious Rhythmic life overflowing with love, greatest joys, vibrant health, sacred ritual, feminine mystery, spiritual connection, and abundance. Learn more about Cindy at www.InHerFullness.com.

Best-selling author, spiritual mentor, and speaker LARA JAYE passionately inspires others to transform themselves to realize their biggest dreams. She teaches her clients how to shine light into their darkest corners, release stale patterns that keep them stuck, and live their unique purpose. In "More Than Enough: Discover Your Limitless Potential and Live Your Bravest Dream," Lara guides others through change. Learn more at LaraJaye.com and to receive your very own copy of her #1 Amazon best-seller.

HEDY MACDONALD, founder of Sacred Soul Gardening, is a spiritual mentor, teacher and energy worker. She guides individuals to access their innate power, trust their inner wisdom, understand their ability to heal and know their divinity. She helps those on a spiritual path align with their higher-self via her writing, individual and group energy alignment sessions and group programs. Connect with her work at www.HedyMacDonald.com.

MARIANNE MACKENZIE is a Radical Coach for business women, the teams they lead, and the men they love. Engaging more deeply is the secret to turning on the joy and passion. When we come from our deepest desires we bring our best-self to everything we do. The power tools and life strategies she teaches bring the idea of Radically Engaged Living™ into practical and sustainable practices. If you desire to create a rewarding relationship with life and your business check out the RēL Woman In Business™ group coaching program at www.MarianneMacKenzie.com.

STACEY MARTINO believes that it only takes *one* partner to transform a relationship ... *any* relationship! She is passionate about helping people create their unshakable love and unleashed passion! Stacey and her husband Paul are the founders of RelationshipDevelopment.org and creators of RelationshipU®. Today, through their strategic coaching, online programs, and packed live events, Stacey and Paul have helped tens of thousands of people around the world transform their love relationships! As a happy bonus, you get to apply the same strategies to improve *all* your relationships. Begin transforming *your* relationships today! Download their free e-book, *It Does Not Take Two to Tango: How to Transform Any Relationship in 8 Simple Steps* at www.RelationshipDevelopment.org.

MICHELLE MERCIER is the CEO/Founder of Create Honesty, a company focused on inspiring and empowering women to create the life they want and not the one they feel they "should" have. She believes every woman has the right to be truly happy and deeply satisfied with her life. Michelle spreads this message through speaking engagements, personal and professional coaching, writing, and interactive workshops. Learn more at www.CreateHonesty.com and download your free "Honest Living Starter Kit."

LIZETE MORAIS embodies her "Authentic Voice" message by empowering professional, executive, and passionate women around the world to expand and transform their lives, their professions, and their intimate relationships. Using powerful principles of awakening, awareness, and authenticity, coupled with her ability to identify the real core issues standing between us and our desires and dreams, Lizete facilitates transformation effortlessly and effectively. You were born to live a life of joy, abundance and unconditional love. Schedule your free Clarity Session at www.AuthenticVoice.co.

Consciously merging her practical tools as a psychologist with her intuitive and spiritual gifts, DR. DEBRA L. REBLE empowers women to connect with their hearts and live authentically through her transformational Soul-Hearted Living™ program. Debra is the author of the international best-selling book *Being Love: How Loving Yourself Creates Ripples of Transformation in Your Relationships and The World* (May 2016) and has coauthored four of ILP's best-selling collaborative books. She lives in Cleveland, OH with her soul partner, Doug, and her dog, Shiloh. Claim Debra's 4-part Soul-Hearted Living Sacred Meditation Series at www.DrDebraReble.com.

ROBIN REID is a gifted intuitive, healer and medium who has worked in both the corporate world and the world of divination and brings a down-to-earth approach to the unseen. Through compassionate listening and divine guidance, Robin facilitates healing at the soul level for women to create big shifts with their most stubborn life issues, access their own guidance and inner wisdom to create the passionate lives they long for. Go to www.RobinAnnReid.com to learn more and download your free report, "Beyond Diet, Exercise and Sleep: 7 Energy Techniques to Heal Your Body."

SHELLEY RIUTTA, MSE, LPC is the founder and President of the Global Association of Holistic Psychotherapy and Coaching. She is a Holistic Psychotherapist and creator of a 6-figure Holistic Psychotherapy practice. Because of her success at creating a thriving Holistic Practice she launched the Global Association of Holistic Psychotherapy and Coaching (GAHP) which supports Holistic Therapists, Healers, Coaches and Health Practitioners to develop Thriving 6 Figure Holistic Practices and learn about Holistic Methods™ to accelerate the results of their clients. Visit www.theGAHP.com to learn more.

Business Mentor and Lifestyle Expert LISA MARIE ROSATI is the Creatrix of The Goddess Lifestyle Plan® and Sugar Free Goddess™, an Expert Columnist for *Aspire Magazine*, an international best-selling author, and High Priestess of The Goddess Lifestyle Sisterhood™ & School of Magical Living. Believing that women *can* have it all, Lisa has created a thriving, global brand that teaches women how to step into their feminine power in each key area of life. It's Lisa's passion to teach ambitious, soulful women how to create an abundant, purpose-filled, vibrant, healthy life, and prosperous laptop business they love! Learn how to manifest your desires by utilizing New Moon energy by downloading Lisa's free gift here: www.GoddessLifestylePlan.com/new-moon-magic!

ANN SANFELIPPO is a #1 international best-selling author, speaker, coach, and founder of The Wealth Attraction Academy, a company dedicated to providing women with the tools and resources they need to manifest an abundant life of their dreams—financially, emotionally and spiritually. She has studied the philosophies of the most powerful influencers in the world, both past and present; these incredible mentors helped propelled her to outstanding success. Now, she shares her formula with the world. Learn more at www.WealthAttractionAcademy.com and download The Wealth Attraction Tool Kit.

CHARISSE SISOU is on a mission: to populate the world with happy women. As High Priestess of Pleasure to Women Here to Change the World and Chief Correspondent from Your Happy Place, she connects women leaders and changemakers with their innate feminine superpowers, magnetic nature and untapped resources through retreats, workshops, and Claim Your Feminine Power course, enabling them to smash glass ceilings and show up whole and holy–curves, edges, and all. Learn more at www.ClaimYourFeminine.com and download your free gift, the "Every Day Pleasure" book and video series.

KIMBERLY TOBIN is a transformation mentor; business strategist, radio show host, author and speaker helping spiritual women clearly acknowledge and embrace their unique gifts that fears often conceal. She is passionate about helping women strengthen their connection to Spirit enabling them to celebrate their Divine inner magic and create the life they boldly desire. Kimberly works virtually with her clients from her office in Missouri offering transformational programs and classes, as well as in person at beautiful locations around the world. Learn more about Kimberly at www.KimberlyTobin.com and download her free gift: "Through Fear to Fabulous—Learning to be You."

KATT TOZIER is a writer, podcast host, and Divine Life Flow Guide. Through a unique combination of intuitive reading and practical guidance, she helps women clear the patterns that keep them trapped and invoke their healing power. Katt is the Founder of Indomitable Women; she believes, as women, our power is in our individuality and our strength is in our unity, and she facilitates gathering spiritual women together to support our collective healing. Learn more at www.IndomitableWomen.org and download Katt's free gift, "The 4 Gateways of Personal Power."

KAILEAN WELSH. MS, LPC is a Holistic Psychotherapist and Wisdom Teacher. Specializing in Practical Spirituality, Kailean is passionate about returning psychotherapy to its roots as "care of the soul." Kailean offers transformational programs, online courses, and live workshops virtually, as well as from her office in Wisconsin. With compassion, connection, and joy, she helps people heal at their core, Illuminate their Best Self, and Shine! Learn more at www.KaileanWelsh.com and download her free gift: "Five Spiritual Truths to Transform Your Life Now."

NICOLE WETTEMANN is a Catalyst for Spiritual and Personal Trans-formation. She helps women be who they need to be to live the life they came here to live. She does this by helping to clear any obstacles that are holding them back from living an authentic, spiritually connected life and by liberating them to step fully into their purpose and bringing their dreams and vision to life through the guidance of their angels and spiritual guides. Learn more at www.NicoleWettemann.com and download your free meditation, "Awakening to your Divinity."

ABOUT THE PUBLISHER

Linda Joy

*F*ounded in 2010 by Inspirational Catalyst, radio show host, and *Aspire Magazine* Publisher Linda Joy, Inspired Living Publishing (ILP) is an international best-selling inspirational boutique publishing company dedicated to spreading a message of love, positivity, feminine wisdom, and self-empowerment to women of all ages, backgrounds, and life paths. Linda's multimedia brands reach over 44,000 subscribers and a social media community of over 24,000 women.

Through our highly-successful anthology division, we have brought eight books and over 300 visionary female authors to best-seller status. Our powerful, high-visibility publishing, marketing, and list-building packages have brought these authors—all visionary entrepreneurs, coaches, therapists, and health practitioners—the positive, dynamic exposure they need to attract their ideal audience and thrive in their businesses.

Inspired Living Publishing also publishes single-author books by visionary female authors whose messages are aligned with Linda's philosophy of authenticity, empowerment, and personal transformation. Recent best-selling releases include the award-winning *Being Love: How Loving Yourself Creates Ripples of Transformation in Your Relationships and the World*, by Dr. Debra L. Reble; and the multiple-award-winning *The Art of Inspiration: An Editor's Guide to Writing Powerful, Effective Inspirational & Personal Development Books*, by ILP Chief Editor Bryna René Haynes.

ILP's family of authors reap the benefits of being a part of a sacred family of inspirational multimedia brands which deliver the best in transformational and empowering content across a wide range of platforms. Our hybrid publishing packages and *à la carte* marketing and media packages provide visionary female authors with access to our proven best-seller model and high-profile multimedia exposure across all of Linda's imprints (including *Aspire Magazine*, the "Inspired Conversations" radio show on OMTimes Radio, the Inspired Living Giveaway, Inspired Living Secrets, and exposure to Linda's loyal personal audience of over 44,000 women).

If you're ready to publish your transformational book, or share your story in one of ours, we invite you to join us! Learn more about our publishing services at www.InspiredLivingPublishing.com.

ABOUT THE EDITOR

Bryna René Haynes, ILP Chief Editor

"Word Alchemist" Bryna René Haynes is the founder of The Heart of Writing, the chief editor for Inspired Living Publishing, and the best-selling author of the multiple-award-winning book, *The Art of Inspiration: An Editor's Guide to Creating Powerful, Effective Inspirational and Personal Development Books* (2016). Her heart-centered book development coaching, editing services, and online courses are designed to help inspired writers move through their blocks and perceived limitations, connect with their authentic voices, and create world-changing written works that transform their lives and businesses.

Bryna's editing portfolio includes numerous successful non-fiction titles, including all of Inspired Living Publishing's best-selling print anthologies.

Through her company, The Heart of Writing, Bryna and her team offer educational tools, online writing courses, creative support and coaching, and professional editing services for authors, business owners, and bloggers in all genres.

Bryna lives outside of Providence, Rhode Island with her husband, Matthew, and their daughters, Áine (aka, Moonbeam) and Aelyn (aka, Little Star). When she's not writing, you can find her teaching yoga philosophy, practicing her landscape photography, and singing her heart out in any place with good acoustics.

Learn more about Bryna, meet The Heart of Writing Team, and access Bryna's ever-expanding free Resource Library at www.TheHeartofWriting.com.

ABOUT THE EDITOR

Deborah Kevin, ILP Associate Editor

Writer, editor, and storyteller Deborah Kevin is the Chief Inspiration Officer of Deborah Kevin, former online editor of *Little Patuxent Review*, and an associate editor for Inspired Living Publishing. She works with heart-centered, service-minded entrepreneurs to confidently share their brilliance on the page, on the web, and in their marketing.

Deborah's portfolio includes ILP's *Courageous Hearts* and several best-selling nonfiction titles. Her essays and interviews have been published by *Aspire Magazine*, *Equitas International*, Karen Salmansohn, and *Little Patuxent Review*.

Through her company, Deborah and her team offer strategic writing and editing packages for entrepreneurs, authors, and bloggers.

Deborah lives outside Baltimore, Maryland with her two sons and their cat, Princess Leia. When she's not writing, Debby can be found hiking, kayaking, dancing, cooking, and traveling.

To learn more about Deborah, visit www.DeborahKevin.com.

Made in the USA
San Bernardino, CA
26 October 2017